THE COLLEGE STUDENT'S GUIDE TO TRANSFERRING SCHOOLS

JENNIFER WILCHA & DAVID A. SMITH

"Wilcha and Smith explain in clear terms
all the technicalities of transferring and offer effective
strategies on how to reapply successfully.
The *Guide*'s Six Step Plan is a
practical approach to switching schools,
and the personal interviews with students
supply the inside story of both trials and tribulations
of transferring.
The College Student's Guide to Transferring Schools
will help you make the most of your second chance."
From the Preface by Edward B. Fiske,
Author of *Fiske Guide to Colleges*,
Education Columnist of *The New York Times*

"WILCHA AND SMITH'S GUIDE IS SENSIBLE,
REALISTIC AND HELPFUL . . .
A MUST READ FOR RESTLESS UNDERGRADUATES."
Theodore Sizer,
Professor of Education,
Brown University

"I WISH I HAD IT WHEN I TRANSFERRED!
USE IT!"
Steve Cohen &
Paulo de Oliveira,
Co-authors of *Getting In*

THE COLLEGE STUDENT'S GUIDE TO TRANSFERRING SCHOOLS

THE HOWs, WHENs AND WHYs OF SWITCHING COLLEGES

JENNIFER WILCHA & DAVID A.SMITH

AVON BOOKS ◭ NEW YORK

To our parents,
for their love, support, and tuition

THE COLLEGE STUDENT'S GUIDE TO TRANSFERRING SCHOOLS is an original publication of Avon Books. This work has never before appeared in book form.

The authors extend their gratitude for permission to reprint an excerpt from *How To Get an Ivy League Education at a State University* by Martin Nemko, Ph.D., copyright © 1988 by Martin Nemko. Used by arrangement with Avon Books.

AVON BOOKS
A division of
The Hearst Corporation
105 Madison Avenue
New York, New York 10016

Copyright © 1990 by Jennifer Wilcha and David A. Smith
Cover photograph copyright © 1990 by Bruce Fritz Photography
Published by arrangement with the authors
Library of Congress Catalog Card Number: 90-93173
ISBN: 0-380-75982-9

Library of Congress Cataloging in Publication Data:

Wilcha, Jennifer.
The college student's guide to transferring schools / Jennifer Wilcha and David A. Smith.
    p.   cm.
Includes bibliographical references and index.
ISBN 0-380-75982-9 (trade)
1. Students, Transfer of—United States—Handbooks, manuals, etc. 2. Transfer students—United States. 3. College, Choice of—United States. 4. Universities and colleges—United States—Directories. I. Smith, David A., 1969-　. II. Title.
LB2360.W55 1990
378.1′69—dc20
90-93173
CIP

First Avon Books Trade Printing: November 1990

AVON TRADEMARK REG. U.S. PAT. OFF. AND IN OTHER COUNTRIES, MARCA REGISTRADA, HECHO EN U.S.A.

Printed in the U.S.A.

OPM 10 9 8 7 6 5 4 3 2 1

ACKNOWLEDGMENTS

Thanks:

To all the transfer students and admissions officers we spoke with and everybody who returned our questionnaires. To Joan Johnson, Lauren Pickard, Pat and John Wilcha, Jason Loewith, Glen Roberts and Sarah Hodges for proofreading. To Samuel Engel for superb investigative reporting, Kevin Barr and Rosemarie Capello for their post-graduation guidance, Robin Woods for sending us everything, and Lynn Hogan for answering all our questions about publishing.

To Serena Kalb, Terry Pope, David Szlag, Gloria Leiberman, and Laurie Reynolds for helping us through the trauma of finding housing. To Lisa Heller, Sharon Cohen, Gabriella Tobal, and the man on the telephone at Microsoft Word for saving us in crises.

To Michael for his patience during printing, Christopher for successfully testing our advice, Melissa Levis and Tim Murpy for knowing how to rhyme, and the most specialist wonderful thanks to Caroline Shirley Hansen.

Thanks also to Brooke Berman, Lianne Manshel, Andrew Shiva, Randa Massot, Alexa Magna, Morgean Milkofsky, Morgan Sturges, Peter Foster, Laurie Goodman, Pablo Hernandez, Mickey McCarthy, and Rebecca Woodruff.

To the American Association of Community & Junior Colleges, the National Collegiate Athletic Association, MIT Air Force ROTC, and Commander Dugen at the Pentagon. To the

Wallachs for setting an example, opening the doors, and calling often from Tunisia.

And most of all, to both our agent, Nina Graybill, and our editor, Judith Riven, for saying yes.

CONTENTS

Breaking Up—Reevaluating the Relationship • A Note
to First-Year Students • Social Life • Academics •
Extracurricular Life • Campus • Questionnaire Scores •
A Last Word

Telling the Folks • Renegotiation—Probable Parental
Reactions • Financial Aid Options • Strategic Financial
Planning • Saying Goodbye to Friends • Transferring
for Love

This Isn't High School Anymore • Getting It *Just Right*
• Playing the Field—Researching Schools • Other
Considerations—ROTC • Visiting—The First Date •
Video Dating

CONTENTS

PREFACE

Some years ago, I received a letter from a friend who described his particular college experience as "a four-year jail term with a sixty-thousand-dollar fine." Unfortunately, he was not alone in this assessment. Many students come home after the first year of college disappointed and dismayed. University life is comprised of a wide variety of elements: academic, social, geographic and extracurricular. If any one of these does not match a student's particular needs, the entire experience may be ruined.

College is a time of extreme transition and as people discover more about themselves their expectations inevitably change. Given the major financial investment that a college education now entails, no one should endure four years of unhappiness. *The College Student's Guide to Transferring Schools* shows students and their parents the alternatives.

The College Student's Guide Six-Step Plan is a practical approach to switching schools. The plan employs the metaphor of a relationship, one that is particularly apt since college is an important four-year commitment. As a result, any major change must begin with a rigorous evaluation of one's self and one's school.

The book offers advice on how to deal with the objections commonly raised by parents and friends, and it provides an extensive discussion of how to find a new school. Wilcha and Smith explain in clear terms all the technicalities of transferring, and they offer effective strategies on how to reapply successfully. Finally, the book addresses the difficulty of readjustment and the unique concerns of junior college students.

Most important, however, are the personal interviews interspersed throughout the book. They supply the inside story of both the trials and tribulations of transferring. Anyone considering changing schools would be wise to find out what their peers have to say about the subject. Reading these students' experiences can help one make a calculated and informed decision about whether or not transferring is appropriate.

In addition to explaining why transferring is a valuable option, *The College Student's Guide* also raises important caveats about the process. Switching schools is rarely easy and it is important to be forewarned of the pitfalls. This book will help you navigate the often treacherous obstacles of arranging transfer credit and housing.

During my many years of reporting on higher education in America, I have found that there are plenty of good schools out there. Don't give up if you did not find a perfect match the first time around. *The College Student's Guide to Transferring Schools* will help you make the most of your second chance.

Edward B. Fiske
Author of the *Fiske Guide to Colleges*
Education Columnist of *The New York Times*

Introduction:
The Six-Step Plan

To live is to change, and to be perfect is to have changed often.
                                    —*John Henry Newman*

For F. Scott Fitzgerald, college was a cocktail party. For Ben Franklin, it was an "education for citizenship." For Flounder Dorfman, it was four years of fraternity. Although the images may vary, the myth remains constant: college is supposed to be the best years of your life.

So what do you do when it isn't? What do you do when professors are lousy, when classes are overwhelming, when parties are scarce? What do you do when you realize that the school you're in is the one that you'd like to get out of? If you chose the wrong school, or never got into the right one, there is no reason you should have to spend four years regretting the past.

Instead, you can transfer. Yet the widespread view of transferring is that it's rare, difficult to do, and used only as a last resort. In fact, one out of five students transfers during his or her college career.[1] If college isn't living up to your expectations, you are not alone.

But how do you know if transferring is the right answer? It certainly takes a lot of time and effort, it means going through the application process all over again, and it means making

---

1. U.S. Department of Labor, 1989.

friends at a new school. Maybe transferring is not right for you. *The College Student's Guide to Transferring Schools* will answer all of your questions about changing schools. When is the best time to transfer? How hard is it to get in? Will you lose credit? What will readjustment be like? This book will give you an honest, objective picture of the pro's and con's of switching schools. In other words, it is a book for anyone who has ever wondered, "Would I be happier somewhere else?"

Each chapter outlines the **Six-Step Plan to Successfully Changing Schools.** Based on interviews with hundreds of admissions officers, transfer students, and college advisors, the **Six-Step Plan** covers every stage of the process from "Breaking Up" to "Starting Over." College is an intimate four-year relationship, and transferring is a lot like breaking up and meeting someone new. It takes Reevaluation, Renegotiation, Research, Reapplication, Revision, and Readjustment. The **Six-Step Plan** is a systematic approach to this potentially overwhelming process.

THE SIX-STEP PLAN TO SUCCESSFULLY CHANGING SCHOOLS

BREAKING UP
Reevaluation

TELLING THE FOLKS
Renegotiation

PLAYING THE FIELD
Research

MAKING THE FIRST MOVE
Reapplication

WRITING THE LOVE LETTER
Revision

STARTING OVER
Readjustment

The book also features special information for junior and community college students, including practical advice on Strategic Financial Planning, choosing a junior college, avoiding transfer shock, and arranging course credit. Plus, it explains the complicated terminology of transferring: from articulation agreements to automatic transfer to concurrent enrollment, *The College Student's Guide to Transferring Schools* shows you how to get the education you deserve.

No one can tell you whether or not to transfer, only give you the information to decide on your own. The dozens of personal stories and experiences included throughout the book present a clear picture of both the advantages and disadvantages of switching schools.

This *Guide* will show you how to use what you already know from one or two years of college to transfer easily and successfully. Wasting four years in the wrong school is a mistake. And of the thousands of colleges in the country, there really is one out there that is just right for you.

**TO TRANSFER
TO TRANSFER NOT
TO TRANSFER
TO TRANSFER NOT
TO TRANSFER
TO TRANSFER NOT
TO TRANSFER**

Chapter 1

"Mom, I Want to Come Home"

THE SIX-STEP PLAN TO SUCCESSFULLY CHANGING SCHOOLS

BREAKING UP
Reevaluation

TELLING THE FOLKS
Renegotiation

PLAYING THE FIELD
Research

MAKING THE FIRST MOVE
Reapplication

WRITING THE LOVE LETTER
Revision

STARTING OVER
Readjustment

September 17 3:00 a.m.

*Just awakened by what sounds like a herd
of migrating cattle in the hallway. So this is
college. It's only the second week of school
and I'm already 500 pages behind in all my
classes. Tonight's dinner looked like it
crawled off the football field and my
roommate's parents call every morning at
6:30 . . .*

I think I hate it here.

At some point during the first year of college everyone thinks
about leaving. All it takes is one particularly bad day.
Suddenly, the food is terrible, classes are boring, and the dorms
definitely don't look like they did in the catalogue. At some
point during the first year, everyone calls: "Mom, I want to
come home."

How unhappy does one have to be to make leaving worthwhile? Not very. Todd Bartlett was hesitant to leave Tufts
because he was afraid he was "not miserable enough." Today
he calls transferring the "best move" of his life. Some reasons
for leaving, however, are more valid than others. The goal of
this chapter is to give you a fresh perspective on your situation.
Is it going to improve after your first year? Or is it going to
remain unpleasant until you graduate four years down the line?
You owe it to yourself to examine carefully what it is that is
making you unhappy and what you can do to change it.

Successful transferring begins by reevaluating your relationship with your school. This self-examination later becomes
crucial in every stage of the process: when confronting your
parents with the decision to transfer, when searching for a
better school, when writing the transfer essay, and finally when
making the transition to a new environment.

Most high school seniors skip this intensive self-evaluation.
But as a transfer it is essential because you no longer have a
guidance counselor to help get you into a good school, you
cannot consult your parents on a day-to-day basis, and you don't
have friends who are going through the same agonizing process.
And, most important, you cannot afford to make any of the
mistakes you made the first time. All this means that choosing
to transfer demands self-discipline, self-examination, and self-
confidence.

BREAKING UP
Reevaluating the Relationship

A relationship requires a lot of work in the beginning, but if you are unfulfilled emotionally, socially, or intellectually, you can't expect it to get better with time. You do not want to be buying books called *Students Who Love Too Much and the Schools Who Hate Them.*

Obviously, if you are dissatisfied, the relationship is not working. Before you decide to call it quits, however, it's only fair to see if things can be improved. First, you must distinguish between intrinsic incompatibility and superficial discontent. Some problems are the result of irreconcilable differences between yourself and your school. Others are difficulties you would face at any college. We are not, however, going to make a list of good versus bad reasons to transfer; no reason is too trivial. It is perfectly reasonable, for example, to transfer because of horrible weather. On the other hand, many problems can be solved without going to the extreme of switching schools. If any aspect of your college experience is making you unhappy, you should change it. The key is to differentiate between the factors you can control and the ones you can't.

Remember, in high school, when you were so overwhelmed by all the things you absolutely had to finish by tomorrow, and you would despair about the trials of being a teenager, Mom would calmly say, "You should make a list"? She was right. Use the questionnaires below to make an honest assessment of yourself and your school.

As you list all of the things about your college that you dislike, make note as well of the things you really appreciate. All too often when people decide to transfer they search only for what their current school lacks, which can lead to later problems. Elizabeth Coine, for example, left Arkansas College for the larger course selection of Tulane University. She soon missed the feeling of safety at Arkansas College, however. "I never realized how much I liked not having to lock my door," Elizabeth said. Often we take for granted the things we appreciate most about a school. You might eventually find it necessary to make a trade-off. (It may simply be worth sacrificing warm weather for the advantages of being in Cambridge.) But at this stage of the game, you need to figure out your ideal situation.

Whether or not you eventually decide to transfer, it is wise to seek some counseling first. Most universities really do want you to be happy, and they often provide institutionalized networks of counselors and advisors. Seek these people out, no matter how trivial you think your problem may be. And don't give up if the first person you talk to is too busy to help. Get references and try again. Breaking up is never easy, and you'll regret it later if you don't take advantage of all the available resources now.

A NOTE TO FIRST-YEAR STUDENTS

Keep in mind that the first year of college is always fraught with problems. Being away from home, living with strangers, eating cafeteria food, and adjusting to the increased workload of college is inevitably stressful. Even if they don't show it, your friends are probably experiencing similar angst. You might want to check out Ronald Farrar's *College 101: Making the Most of Your Freshman Year* (Princeton, NJ: Peterson's Guides, 1988), which answers many commonly asked questions about college life. Addressed to parents, *Letting Go* (Bethesda, MD: Adler & Adler, 1988) by Karen Coburn also provides valuable insight into the first year of college.

But after the first month's transition, the hardships shouldn't outweigh the pleasures. Investigate upperclass life at your school. Nevertheless, don't just go by the advice of a few junior or senior friends. Someone who has already devoted three years to a school may feel compelled to say nice things about it. On the other hand, some seniors just make a habit of complaining. Get facts: about housing, about classes, about extracurricular opportunities. Not only will a thorough investigation of your school prove invaluable if you decide to transfer, it will make your remaining years much more enjoyable if you decide to stay.

SOCIAL LIFE

Community

"Diversity is the hallmark of the Harvard/Radcliffe experience" reads the opening line of the Harvard admissions brochure. Today, almost every college emphasizes the variety and plurality of its student population. But despite the enthusiasm of much advertising, some schools are simply less successful at attracting a wide range of students than others. As you begin your self-evaluation, consider the community at your present school. Do you find it comfortable? Would you hope to find the same groups of people at a new school?

When you were selecting a college the first time around, you may not have been aware of the importance of a diverse student population, or you may have been misled by a school's advertising campaign. Jeremy Stuart found the students at Lehigh "too white and too wealthy," so he transferred to Sarah Lawrence. Meanwhile, Kanji Feldman left Boston College because "there weren't enough bi-racial students," and he felt out of place. Emily Richardson left Rutgers because "It was too much like high school. Everyone was from New Jersey." A homogeneous student population is a very common reason for transferring.

But diversity is not for everyone. There's nothing wrong with wanting to go to a school with people from your own background. As a southern black student you may not want to attend a predominantly white school in the North for your first years away from home. As Lynnea Walker said after spending a visiting year away from Tougaloo, "In the South there are racists and you know who they are. They don't talk to you, and you don't talk to them. But up north you can't tell who's who. It's a scary feeling." Nor do you need to be in an environment where your political values or religious beliefs will be constantly attacked. College is a place where you should feel comfortable enough to succeed. Jacklyn Thompson did well at Trinity but felt like a "lonesome, misplaced Texan among New England prep schoolers." She transferred to Vanderbilt and is much happier in Tennessee. Alicia McGowan, who transferred to Simmons, said, "I like the atmosphere of an all-female environment. I just fit in a lot better."

Indeed, many studies have shown that women tend to perform better in single-sex than in co-educational schools.[1] They participate more in class, have greater self-confidence, and get better jobs upon graduating. One year away from the security of high school may radically change your feelings about community. If you initially were tempted to try a diverse environment and now you know it's not right for you, transferring is a valid option. Don't be tricked by the current media campaign; diversity is not a guarantee for happiness.

1. *Men and Women Learning Together: A Study of College Students in the Late 1970's.* Report of the Brown Project, April 1980.

Entertainment

When you were searching for a college in high school, the prospect of total freedom may have clouded your vision about the realities of college life. And if your parents helped you choose a school, they might not have been too concerned about your chances of getting a date on a Saturday night. On the one hand, it would have been hard to convince them (or yourself) that you did not want to go to an Ivy League school because you were afraid everyone spent all their time in the library. On the other, it would have been very risky to choose a school for its "party" reputation. But college is supposed to be fun (isn't it?). If you feel isolated, lonely, or bored, something is not right.

Before you can justify to yourself, or to your parents, the need to find a school with a better social scene, you need to analyze carefully the problems with your present one. Is it that there's nothing to do on weekends or that you hate everything that's offered? Is there really no dating on campus or does everybody just like to whine? We all tend to generalize about our schools— "the people are shallow, there's nothing to do, the parties are stupid." Before you leave because you're bored with the people you know, think about how difficult it's going to be to make friends at a new school. If you transfer as a junior or even a sophomore, most people will already have formed close groups of friends.

The presence of fraternities, the quality of campus-sponsored events, and the availability of local theater and entertainment, all shape the way you feel about a school. Yet as a high school student it may have been impossible to predict what your interests would be in college. Before even graduating high school, Will Cutter assumed he would join a fraternity. But during "pledging," he realized Greek life had not lived up to his expectations. Nor was he satisfied with the other elements of the Northwestern social scene, so he transferred to the University of Virginia. UVA has a strong Greek system as well, but Will says he feels a greater sense of community as an "independent" at the southern school than he did at Northwestern.

Obviously the location of your school will largely dictate the opportunities for escape from campus. Again, before you decide to leave the countryside for the excitement of the city, consider all the disadvantages: the higher cost of living, the difficulty of finding housing, and the common feeling of isolation that exists in large cities.

The first year can be especially difficult on your social life. To find out if the situation will get better with time, do some hard-core investigation. Are seniors generally happy, or do they groan endlessly as well? If your school offers psychological counseling, ask a counselor for his or her perspective on the college. Problems you experience may indeed be endemic to the school. An unbalanced male-to-female ratio may not seem like a problem in the course catalogue, but dating is hard enough as it is.

Political Climate

Community and social life are both affected by the political climate of your school. It is easy to feel isolated as the lone Republican on a Marxist campus. Some may find this a challenge; you may find it unbearable. Many students apply to college the first time without knowing their own particular political bent. If you just discovered your political identity, the school you chose originally may now be the wrong one.

By the same token, you may find that your school is intolerant of your sexual identity. Or you may just want to start over at another university. One student transferred from Purdue because "everyone thought of me as heterosexual—'coming out' there would have been too difficult." Again, it is important to decide exactly what you are looking for in a new school. Do you want just a large lesbian and gay population or a politically active community?

Religion

After leaving home for the first time, students often discover they miss the religious community they took for granted growing up. When Matthew Weinstein went to Stanford, he didn't expect to mind the lack of "Jewish culture and customs" at the university. Nor did he anticipate the difficulties of keeping kosher on the West Coast. "I couldn't find anything to eat. Everything out there is Mexican—milk and meat together." He transferred to the University of Pennsylvania for its large Jewish population and kosher meal plan. For information about Jewish life on campus, try Dr. Lee and Lana Goldberg's *The Jewish Student's Guide to American Colleges* (New York: Shapolsky Publishers, 1989).

Several students we spoke with transferred because they wanted to leave schools with strong religious affiliations. Emma Sturgis left St. Anselm's to escape the "parietal" system. Every time a student was caught in a dorm of the opposite sex after hours, he or she was fined for the infraction. Kristin Webster left Providence College for the same reason. "We had to pay one dollar a minute we spent in someone else's room. It was fifty dollars if you were caught with a beer. Dorm parties were always illegal and then the school started clamping down on off-campus parties, too." Both women said they were uninformed about the extent of the parietal systems when they applied. "I knew they were strict, but not that strict," says Kristin.

Finally . . .

If you are planning on transferring and the social life at your school is satisfactory, make sure when picking a new one that it offers similar opportunities. When you are unhappy it is easy to ignore the abundance of cheap entertainment or the late-night quiet of the dorm halls. What do you like about your present school? What would you want to change? In order to convince yourself, and your parents, that a bad social life is worth transferring, it is important to be specific and thorough in your examination.

Top Ten Things You Can Change Without Leaving

1. Your roommate
2. Your grades
3. Your classes
4. Your major
5. Your weight
6. Your image
7. Your friends
8. Your sex life
9. Your meal plan
10. Your attitude

Social Life Survey

Circle appropriate response.

STUDENTS

Not Enough...		Too Much...	
	artists		pretentiousness
	athletes		school spirit
	intellectuals		pseudo-intellectualism
	scientists		
	people like me		studying
			homogeneity

SEX

Not Enough...		Too Much...	
	dating		pressure
	casual romance		sleeping around
	good choices		whining
	experimentation		perversity

GREEK LIFE

Not Enough...		Too Much...	
	free beer		throwing up
	parties		bad music
	real guys		male bonding

Not Enough...		Too Much...	
	social events		makeup
	sisterhood		cattiness
	old-fashioned girls		pink

OFF CAMPUS

Not Enough...		Too Much...	
	bars		drinking
	entertainment		distraction
	night life		noise

COMMUNITY

Not Enough...		Too Much...	
	religion		proselytizing
	gay awareness		homosexuality
	feminism		liberalism
	Third World unity		separatism

ACADEMICS

In a transfer application, academic dissatisfaction is the most persuasive reason for wanting to change schools. Whether you feel your college is too hard, too easy, or does not offer the subjects which interest you, your chances of getting admitted are highest if you are transferring for academic reasons. So, even if you really want to get out because your social life is nonexistent, reevaluate your academic situation. Are you being intellectually challenged? Are the professors excellent in your department? If not, make note of it. When it comes time to write the transfer essay, you can't just complain about the weather.

If you do want to transfer primarily for academic reasons, make sure the school to which you apply will fulfill your needs. Many students find that their interests and goals change after a year or two at college. Although Alice Hooks was very happy socially at Vanderbilt, she wanted to study broadcast journalism, a major not offered by the school. She felt she was making an important "career decision" by transferring to Boston University, renowned for its Communications Department. Changing schools may not always be necessary, however; many colleges sponsor academic exchange programs, as well as independent study opportunities and internships in professional fields. One or more of these options, which are detailed in Chapter 6, may suit your needs and save you the hassle of transferring.

For a number of students, however, college course work is simply too hard or too easy. But before you put yourself through the whole application process again, take a deep breath. What exactly is wrong? Is it the level of the courses you're taking? Is it that you are not used to being in large lecture classes? Is it the grading policies of your school or of particular instructors? A school that is easy for you may be hard for somebody else, and not just because the classes are more difficult. A student who prefers anonymity in the classroom is going to be more successful at a large university than a small college. The same rigorous courses at a school where you only take four classes a semester rather than five will be much "easier" academically. It is essential to determine what is unsatisfactory about this school so that you can pick your next one accordingly.

Since much, or most, of what you learn in college occurs outside the classroom and usually after midnight, the quality of a school's students is just as important as that of its faculty. Ben Russel described the people at William Paterson as "unstimulating, unmotivated, and only interested in getting a degree." He transferred to Sarah Lawrence because he felt its progressive curriculum, which emphasizes independent study and tutorial instruction, attracted "more serious intellectual students."

After some reflection, you may realize that you don't want to leave at all. Janie Stowers, a first-year student at American University, decided to stay after consulting her academic advisor. The advisor helped her choose a major and recommended several excellent professors. Even if you stay, reevaluation will help you get better grades, find more accessible professors, and feel more academically fulfilled.

Whatever you do, get to know your professors. They are an excellent resource for learning about your own and other schools. If you do transfer, you will need to have at least two professors who know you well enough to write strong recommendations. Go to their office hours, talk to them after class, ask them out for coffee. They will be impressed with your enthusiasm, and you will find the work much more interesting. Unfortunately, the best subject in the world is sure to be painful if the professor cannot teach, so try to find out *before* registration which professors have good reputations. Ask seniors who are majoring in the department to recommend the best teachers and classes.

If you are not feeling academically challenged, find out if honors programs exist or if it is possible to get into upper-level seminars. Speak with a dean; administrators are always willing to help students who want to work. Be wary of departmental reputations. One famous professor can give an entire department a good or bad name. Then again, he or she may never teach undergraduate courses.

Finally, if you decide to remain at your present school and the work is too difficult, investigate your school's tutoring services. Many universities provide writing centers where you can have someone proofread your papers and workshops to help you study more efficiently. Again, talk to your professors. For a new approach to studying take a look at *Use Both Sides of Your Brain* by Tony Buzan (New York: E. P. Dutton, 1983) or *The Other Way to Better Grades* by Marvin Karlins (New York: Fawcett Columbine, 1981). For a more traditional approach, there's *Barron's Study Tips: How to Study Effectively & Get Better Grades,* by William Armstrong and M. Willard Trampe (Woodbury, NY: Barron's Educational Series, 1983). And to get the most for your money, try *How to Get an Ivy League Education at a State University* by Martin Nemko (New York: Avon Books, 1988).

Academic Assessment

	Amazing	Interest-ing	Decent	Under-whelming	Heinous
Professors					
Accessibility					
Teaching Ability					
Scholarship					
Graduate TAs					
Departments					
Structure					
Size					
Quality					
Facilities					
Classes					
Size					
Competition					
Variety					
Availability					
Majors					
Advising					
Choice					
Requirements					
Flexibility					

EXTRACURRICULAR LIFE

In high school you may have been the editor of your yearbook, the star pitcher on the baseball team, or the lead in most school plays; don't panic if you meet rejection at college for the first time. Seniority is a reality at every school.

On the other hand, if you are interested in acting but you don't want to be a Theater major and you find out that one has to be in the department to audition, that is a valid reason to transfer. Likewise, you shouldn't have to major in Journalism to write for the school newspaper. Always try to keep in mind what life will be like as a sophomore or a junior. But if you are going to have to wait to be a senior to do things you want, that may be three years too long.

Extracurricular activities reflect deeper truths about a college: the types of students who go there, the support of the administration toward student groups, and the value the school places on learning outside of the classroom. Playing on a team or being in a singing group makes you feel more a part of your school, allows you to meet people with your own interests (especially upperclass students), and gives you a sense of purpose. If you are considering transferring and you are not currently active in one organization or another, give some thought to "getting involved."

But if you are miserable *and* in the band, think carefully about what organizations you would want to participate in at another school. It is easy to overlook the availability of school-sponsored activities. If you are on a team, see Chapter 4 about the various rules and regulations governing transfer athletes.

Extracurricular Evaluation

School-sponsored activities outside of class (e.g., newspaper, radio) are:
- (a) boring
- (b) exciting
- (c) too competitive
- (d) irrelevant

Drugs and alcohol are:
- (a) too prevalent
- (b) too difficult to get
- (c) neither here nor there

Political activism is:
- (a) too left
- (b) too right
- (c) too moderate
- (d) nonexistent
- (e) not an issue

Athletics are:
  (a) not respected
  (b) too important
  (c) too competitive
  (d) lousy
  (e) none of the above

Arts are:
  (a) underfunded
  (b) unavailable
  (c) too elitist

CAMPUS

What specific characteristics, services, programs, and facilities do you want and need in a college? When applying the first time, you probably asked yourself general questions like "Do I want a small college or a large university, an urban or a rural setting, East or West Coast?" You might even have gotten a computer printout from a guidance counselor with a list of schools you were most compatible with. The problem is that such categories are so broad and vague that they become meaningless. Buffalo, Nashville, and San Francisco are all considered urban. As a transfer candidate your concerns should be more directed, detailed, and refined. You need to be specific about what kind of city you mean when you say urban and why you want to be there. What are your priorities? No matter how much you like other aspects of the school, are you going to be miserable because there's nowhere to dance in New Haven?

In addition to location, the size of a school profoundly influences how you experience college. The issue is not, however, as simple as small colleges versus large universities. Most state schools have specialized colleges within the university. Their students have the advantages of personal academic attention and the resources and variety of a larger institution. Likewise, many small colleges participate in consortiums which offer exchange programs, study abroad, and cross registration at nearby schools. You should be aware of these options before rejecting a school as too limited or constricting. Size, is after all, relative. While a school of a thousand students is usually considered "small," you could not possibly meet and get to know every one of those students in four years. And there is always the new class of 250 that arrives each September. There are definite advantages and disadvantages on both ends of the spectrum. Again, you have to be clear about your preferences and priorities.

Weather is often considered a frivolous reason for transferring. But Bryan Young, who transferred from Northwestern to the University of Southern California, described to us what winter was like in Chicago. "It was so windy, the corner newspaper stands were blowing down the street. The tears in my eyes literally turned to icicles." We give that a 10 on the misery index. If the climate is affecting your mood, your grades, or your social life, consider it a perfectly justifiable reason for leaving. You just may not want to write about it in your essay, however (see Chapter 5).

No matter how definite your plans for the future were in high school, they will probably be modified if not radically altered in college. Students frequently change their minds, majors, and life goals. Shifting priorities midstream is a major source of transferring. Use your year or two of college perspective to determine which features your school has that you want to keep and which you absolutely want to change. "Campus" is a broad category. The following list will help you compare your school's specific strengths and weaknesses rather than merely cataloguing its flaws.

Campus Check List

	Current School (good, bad, okay)	Utopia University (change, don't change)
Size		
Location		
Weather		
Physical Appearance		
Distance from Home		
Housing—dorms		
Housing—off campus		
Food		
Health Services		
Building Accessibility		
Academic Facilities		
classroom		
computer		
laboratory		
language lab		
library		
Art Facilities		
art studio		
dance		
music		
theater		
Athletic Facilities		
baseball		
basketball		
crew		
cross country		
diving		
field hockey		
football		
gymnastics		
ice hockey		
lacrosse		
racquet sports		
soccer		
softball		
other		

QUESTIONNAIRE SCORES

So, should you transfer or not? We don't know. There is no score that says "transfer immediately," or one that says "stay where you are." For some, a bad social life is just the price of a good education. For others, it is a waste of youth. We designed each questionnaire to help you think systematically about every aspect of college life. If a lousy social life is the problem, you need to know specifically why you are dissatisfied. More important, what would make it better? You can't run *away from* a bad school, you have to run *to* a good one.

Use these questionnaires to identify what you are looking for in the "perfect" school. Remember, "perfect" is different for everybody. In Chapter 3, you will start searching for the school of your dreams: its campus, academics, extracurricular opportunities, and social life. Before you can find this ideal institution, you need to make concrete assessments of your present situation.

All of the transfers we spoke with advised trusting your instincts. If your gut reaction is that "this school is just not right," that is a good enough reason to transfer, but it is only a beginning. The ivy is always greener somewhere else. You can never be sure if leaving will solve your problems unless you have thoroughly reevaluated your relationship with your school.

A LAST WORD

College is a place to keep warm between high school and an early marriage.
—George Gobel

Most students in England and France never attend what we would call a liberal arts college. Directly after high school the majority of students enroll in either vocational or professional school. In America, a college education has become a rite of passage for anyone who can afford it. But few American college

The Nature and Purpose
of the University

is to find ...

☐ Intellectual fulfillment
☐ Academic challenge
☐ Meaningful employment
☐ Well-paid employment
☐ Spiritual enlightenment
☐ Self-discipline
☐ A transition between high school and "the real world"
☐ A wife
☐ A husband
☐ A life partner
☐ Emotional growth
☐ Psychological stability
☐ Four years of freedom without responsibility
☐ Knowledge
☐ Wisdom
☐ Cultural literacy
☐ Love
☐ Sex
☐ Companionship
☐ Fraternity
☐ Sorority
☐ Parties
☐ Beer
☐ Political consciousness
☐ Empowerment
☐ Prestige
☐ Culture
☐ Social mobility
☐ Identity
☐ Purpose
☐ Friends
☐ Contacts
☐ A vocation
☐ An avocation
☐ A diploma

students ever seriously ask themselves what they hope to get out of their education. Why are *you* in college? Making the decision to transfer is much easier if you know what you're ultimately looking for. What do you expect to get out of higher education? Did you go to college because it seemed like a good idea at the time or was it a strategic long-term investment? Your reasons may be personal, political, or financial. But regardless of the rhetoric about why you *should* be in college, why are you really there?

To Transfer, To Transfer Not—the decision is ultimately yours. Nobody can tell you whether or not to change schools. But by now, you should have a better idea of which problems can be solved by transferring and which cannot. The better you understand your own situation now, the better you will be able to communicate it to your parents, your friends, the professors who will be writing your recommendations, and the admissions officers who will be reading your application.

But even if you are sure that your misery is due completely to intrinsic incompatibility between yourself and your school, transferring may still not be worth the time and effort it requires. As you read the rest of this book, try to get a sense of what it takes to change schools successfully. Learn what objections you may face from your parents and friends. Find out whether or not you are prepared to devote the time necessary to research another school. Compare your own situation with the experiences of other transfer students. Most important, study Chapter 6 on readjustment, the hardest part of the entire process. Starting over at a new school is never easy; the trials of arranging transfer credit and making new friends may convince you to stay put. Every single person we interviewed said in one way or another, "Before you transfer, think twice."

LINDA WAGNER
Connecticut College—Stanford University

Linda Wagner thinks everyone should transfer. "People who have transferred feel closer to the college they change to. They see the real differences between schools and appreciate all the good things more."

In Linda's case, it was her parents who first recognized that she should change schools. "They saw that something was drastically wrong. I had become completely unanimated." And although Linda knew she wasn't happy at Connecticut College, she thought it was "just life." Her parents disagreed.

Linda seriously began to consider transferring after reading a Time *article her mother gave her on genetic research at Stanford. She wanted to be a biology major but had felt limited by Connecticut College's department. Not quite convinced that transferring was the answer, she consulted her academic advisor. He had received his Ph.D. at Stanford, said it would be "the perfect school" for Linda, and offered to write her recommendation.*

Linda made a concerted effort to keep her application positive. "You always have the desire to condemn the school you're at," she said, "and I had very, very negative feelings about Connecticut College, but didn't allow myself to put that into the essay." Instead, Linda focused on her desire to study molecular genetics, an area not offered by her first school. She knew Stanford was renowned for its excellent science program and extensive research facilities. Linda also discussed how she was feeling unchallenged academically and emphasized that she was looking for a more rigorous curriculum.

Linda was accepted mid-year and arrived never having seen the campus. When asked about the risk of not visiting, she said, "I knew it had to be better than Connecticut College." Luckily, Linda loved Stanford immediately. Adjusting was easy because everyone was "so friendly and knocked on my door and introduced themselves." She met people in study sessions, through frequent dorm meetings, and while acting in plays. Linda's roommate was a transfer, from the quarter before, and also helped her get acquainted with the school. Because she had to fulfill Stanford's core requirements, Linda got to know many first-year students. "It worked out great because I stayed an extra year for my master's and we all graduated together."

Linda soon realized that she liked quarters much better than semesters. The accelerated pace prevented her from ever being bored. "A semester seemed to go on forever, but with quarters I felt pressed the whole time." At Connecticut College, Linda found she could get away without doing any work until the last few weeks, but at Stanford she had to study consistently throughout the term.

Stanford accepted all of Linda's credits, and she ended up a quarter ahead. The university even let Linda decide which of their courses she could skip. "I would go to the first few lectures of a class to figure out if I had already learned the material. They let me out of anything I thought was a repeat."

In addition to academics, Linda spent a lot of her time doing theater. She had not acted at all her first year because "at Connecticut College I got the impression that if you weren't a major, you couldn't get a part." Linda found Stanford's atmosphere more welcoming and always felt encouraged to try everything the school offered.

Ultimately, Linda accepts responsibility for her disappointing first year. "My expectations were vague in high school, and I should have applied differently." She made a full assessment of her needs the second time around: "I asked myself what I wanted, and the answer was exciting coursework and challenging classes. So I applied to a school that felt academically like I did." Linda's advice to other students is to decide as early as possible. "The sooner you make the move, the easier everything becomes."

Linda is presently getting her Ph.D. in Biochemistry at the University of Chicago and has just published her first novel. In retrospect, she considers transferring "the single best thing I've ever done."

Chapter 2

Transference
(or, A Little
Pop Psychology on Leaving)

THE SIX-STEP PLAN TO SUCCESSFULLY CHANGING SCHOOLS

BREAKING UP
Reevaluation

TELLING THE FOLKS
Renegotiation

PLAYING THE FIELD
Research

MAKING THE FIRST MOVE
Reapplication

WRITING THE LOVE LETTER
Revision

STARTING OVER
Readjustment

*Our transfer students are good. They know
what they want and they perform at or
beyond the academic level of their former
institutions. They are more diverse than our
native freshman population. And so much
more interesting.*
—*Joseph Carver, Dean of Admissions,
Babson College*

College transferring began at the turn of the century. Before
that time an occasional student may have changed schools, but
it was not until the advent of junior colleges in the early 1900s
that transferring became a formal, standardized process. Junior
colleges allowed students, for the first time, to complete their
general education in two years. Graduates were expected but
not required to continue their education at a senior institution
for specialized study.[1] Still, transferring from one four-year
school to another did not become a common practice until the
1960s, with the growth of community colleges. In the sixties
and seventies, transferring was the only way for a woman to
attend an all-male college.

Today, the popular conception of transferring is that it is
rare, difficult to do, and resorted to only in extreme cases of
personal duress. Yet, one out of every five students transfers
during their college career, and countless more will tell you
that they have contemplated leaving. So why is transferring
perceived as such a mysterious process? Because colleges and
universities have a vested interest in preventing students from
leaving. They want to avoid high attrition rates and poor
publicity. As one admissions officer from Hamilton, a school
with very few transfers, said, "If I had my druthers, I would
get rid of the transfer program altogether." So why don't
schools get rid of it?

Money. The number of transfer applicants a school will admit
varies according to its attrition rate that particular year. When
students take time off, study abroad, or drop out, a school is left
with extra beds. Colleges and universities also admit transfers
to fill gaps in academic departments, athletic teams, and other
school-sponsored activities. When applicant pools started to drop
in 1989, Dartmouth, the only school in the Ivy League not to

1. Thomas Diener, *Growth of an American Invention: A Documentary
History of the Junior and Community College Movement* (Westport, CT: Green-
wood Press, 1986).

accept transfer students on a regular basis, began readmitting them to cut financial losses.

Schools may be forced to *admit* transfers, but they don't have to help those trying to leave. Students who want to transfer from a school will find very little information about how to get out. And to make things more difficult, most schools don't even publish transfer brochures for students who want to get in. In the end, transferring requires a great deal of independence and responsibility.

But even the most independent student needs the support of his or her parents before changing schools. Understandably, many parents are hesitant about advocating such a major move.

TELLING THE FOLKS

When you tell them that you are considering reapplying, you can't expect your parents to be thrilled. Their immediate reaction will probably be, "Didn't you do that already and wasn't it hard enough the first time?" And when they say *you*, they also mean *we*. The degree of their dismay will be directly proportional to how much time, energy, and emotional commitment they invested in getting you into college the first time. If they pored through course catalogues, went on all the tours, and worked diligently to help you find Utopia University, you can imagine their disappointment when it's not as perfect as it seemed.

Since your parents have not experienced your daily life, it is your job to explain your misery in specific, easily understood terms. Imagine if you told your parents you were getting a divorce. They would not only be shocked, they would fear the worst for your future. If there were any chance that you would be moving back home, they might even fear the worst for their own. Your original agreement with your parents was that you were going to go to college for four straight years. Now, you will have to renegotiate those terms.

Understand that your parents' immediate concerns will be different from yours. They may fear an increased financial burden, or want to shield you from double rejection. Moreover, they are familiar with all of the drawbacks of transferring: the difficulty of making new friends, the problems of arranging transfer credit, and the general angst that comes from leaving one place and starting over at another. They will almost inevitably take a pessimistic stance and play "devil's advocate" to all your arguments.

In any event, it would be extremely difficult to transfer without your parents' support. In times of stress you will need their love and understanding, and if they are the ones paying your bills, they have a right to be involved in the decision. For that reason, it is best to consult your parents after finishing this book. Then you will be more prepared to deal respectfully with their anxieties and concerns. Whatever they do say, listen carefully and try to empathize with their position. They are worried about you. But chances are that if you have been unhappy for a while, your parents will already know, and they will try to be as supportive as possible.

It is up to you to decide whether or not you want to consult your parents about transferring before or after choosing a new school. Only you know how your parents will react. If you have not thoroughly researched your new school (as outlined in Chapter 3), however, we suggest not telling your parents you have chosen one. If, on the other hand, you are thinking about transferring to their *alma mater,* tell them. You need all the support you can get. Just remember that any claims you make to your parents (about how unhappy you are, how happy you will be, etc.) need evidence. So if you skipped the self-evaluation in Chapter 1, go back and begin again. Transferring is always about starting over.

RENEGOTIATION
Probable Parental Reactions and Possible Responses to Them

We want you to be happy and the decision is ultimately yours.

It's all downhill from here.

It's terrible that you're unhappy, but it will get better with time. Stick it out for one more year and you'll see.

If you've done your homework, you will be prepared with a list of concrete reasons why it won't get better and that waiting might actually make your situation worse. Show them that you have given your school a fair chance.

Gabrielle Semo was immediately dissatisfied with Columbia, but she attributed her discontent to freshman year, which "is hard for everybody." After returning, she realized that the problem was Columbia and not adjustment to college life. Her advice: "It's hard to do something different than everybody you know, but if you're still unhappy by May, don't go back sophomore year."

Everyone feels that way at college. Why don't you take time off and go abroad for a semester or get a job?

Have you considered these alternatives? Almost all schools offer foreign study programs, and a semester or a year abroad may be better than transferring. Jennifer Michener "needed time away" from Colby, so when she wasn't accepted as a transfer at her first-choice school, she spent her junior year in London. Now she is looking forward to going back to Colby as a senior, and she is glad she didn't have to start over somewhere new.

The possibilities for taking time off are numerous. Information on guest semesters, the Venture program, and employment opportunities is included in Chapter 6. If you decide to take time off, however, and you think you may still want to transfer after you return, make sure that you spend your time wisely. An admissions officer will look twice at any leave of absence on your record.

If you are sure that taking time off is equivalent to prolonging your misery, present your parents with the research and self-examination you have done to support your position.

Top Ten List of Famous Transfers

Woody Allen
NYU to CUNY

Amy Carter
Brown to the Memphis College of Art

Arsenio Hall
Ohio State University to Kent State

Jesse Jackson
University of Illinois to North Carolina A&T

John Kennedy
Princeton to Harvard

John Malkovich
Eastern Illinois University to Illinois State

Edgar Allan Poe
University of Virginia to West Point

Booth Tarkington
Purdue to Princeton

Alice Walker
Spelman to Sarah Lawrence

Woodrow Wilson
Davidson to Princeton

I knew that school wasn't right for you from the beginning. You should be at . . .

If you haven't yet picked a new school, all you want right now is for your parents to agree that transferring is a good idea. Later, you can sell them on whatever school you are most interested in. Always assure them that you will seriously consider their suggestions. If your parents are paying, the least you can do is consult them.

If you have already chosen a new school, explain that you *have* considered the college they recommend, and tell them why you like it. Then illustrate the school's drawbacks and discuss with them the various reasons you have selected the one you did. The more thought out and detailed your reasons, the better your chances of convincing your parents that you made the right choice.

Of course, sometimes it's not that easy. When Leslie St. John transferred to Fairfield, her father thought it was just a stage. But Leslie loved her new school and adamantly refused to return to Smith, which she had "completely hated." Her father was equally adamant that Smith was a better school and would open more doors for her in the future. The issue has been a constant source of conflict and the battle is far from resolved. "Dad thinks I'm going to Smith. I think I'm going to Fairfield. Pretty soon we have to have it out."

Your parents want what is best for you, and it's natural for them to be excited about the prospects of your attending a more prestigious school. But be careful that they're not pushing you—to transfer or to stay where you are. You are the one who has to uproot yourself, find another school, and make new friends. Adjusting will be doubly difficult if you were never sure you wanted to transfer in the first place.

But it's so much trouble. You don't really want to go through all that application stuff again, do you? It won't be worth the aggravation.

Transferring *is* a lot of trouble. To make it worthwhile you have to be clear about your needs and goals. Students who know why they are leaving and what they are looking for in a new school are the most successful transfers. Compare yourself with the profiles featured throughout this book. They represent a wide range of experiences, and highlight some pitfalls you might not have considered. Thoroughly weigh the advantages of changing schools with the disadvantages of starting over before approaching your parents. If you have convinced yourself, you should be able to persuade them.

Regardless, don't count on enthusiasm. Your parents' job was to get you into college and out of the house. They fulfilled their responsibility, so the rest is up to you. Assure them that transferring is a personal decision and that you are prepared to do all the work alone. What you need from them is *moral* support, and a little faith that, yes, it can be worth it.

Transferring is sure to hurt your chances of getting into graduate school.

If anything, transferring will help your chances of getting into graduate school. That is, if your grades are currently low, and you think you can do better at another college. Many graduate schools only ask for your final transcript. Others, however, do ask for your transcripts from both undergraduate schools. Nevertheless, an admissions counselor at the Stanford Law School assured us that "transferring itself never counts against you."

If you are transferring from a highly selective school to one that is less selective, you may want to include a short explanation of your decision with your graduate school application. Indeed, the Harvard School of Arts and Sciences includes a special space on its application "to explain anything that looks unusual" in your academic history. If you are concerned, call the admissions office of any graduate school that you think you might want to attend.

College is supposed to be difficult; you should finish what you start.

Your parents may just not understand the process. They, and everyone else they knew, went through four years at one school, so why can't you? They may mistakenly view transferring as a sign of immaturity and fickleness. Emphasize instead that your decision to transfer requires a great deal of maturity and self-direction. Show them how carefully and systematically you have thought through your situation. Describe your educational goals, so that your parents can see clearly how you are planning to achieve them. Remind your parents that once you graduate, the only school on your diploma is the one in which you finished your education, so that nobody, including future employers, need ever know that you transferred.

Transferring is too competitive. Why do you want to set yourself up for double rejection?

In many schools, the ratio of the number of transfers who apply to the number admitted is the same as for their first-year students. But some schools do accept a much higher proportion of transfer students, and some much lower. Knowing your odds of admission is an important part of researching a new college. Check the Appendix—we have included admissions statistics for each school listed. If the college to which you want to apply is not profiled, call and ask an admissions officer what is the percentage of accepted transfer students.

Parents often fear the blow of "double rejection" if their child wants to transfer to the college he or she was rejected from in high school. We asked many admissions officers if being denied admission once increases an applicant's chances of getting denied a second time, and they unanimously said no. In fact, as one admissions officer at Colgate College said, "We like the people who continue to like us."

Persistence can often help, but it won't guarantee success. Justin Kramer applied to Columbia as a first-year student, was denied, appealed the decision to no avail, took summer classes at Columbia, reapplied as a transfer, and still did not get accepted. Meanwhile, Justin was admitted as a transfer to both Vassar and Duke. Better than persistence is strategy: the following chapters show you how to target the school of your choice through smart research and shrewd reapplication.

It would certainly be wise, before you reapply, to have your high school guidance counselor find out from the college why you were originally denied admission. See Chapter 3, however, for reasons why applying to your first-choice school again may not be such a good idea.

Double rejection is hard to face. Make sure you are prepared to accept it. Tell your parents the truth about your odds of admission; they will be more supportive if things don't turn out the way you had hoped.

You'll have the same problems somewhere else.

Many people do. It is often difficult to gain enough perspective on your own situation to see whether college is the source, or merely a symptom, of your unhappiness. Transferring may not be the answer. Maybe the problem is college in general, and you should not be spending four years trying to get a degree at all. In that case, you have a lot of thinking to do about why you're there and what you hope to get out of higher education.

But if you have thoroughly evaluated your own school and your own goals, you should have a good idea of the source of your unhappiness and how to change it. Andrew Hoffman's parents disapproved of his decision to transfer to Sarah Lawrence. They insisted that it was still a "girls' school." Andrew showed them brochures and pamphlets from the college, as well as guidebooks describing the school, until finally he was able to convince them otherwise. "Do everything you can to prove your case," Andrew said, "and don't give up."

Of course you can transfer, but not to anywhere more expensive than your present school.

For some people this response is as good as a no. But regardless of your specific situation, be glad that your parents are being honest about money before you have invested too much time in the transfer process. Since financial factors will greatly affect your research in Chapter 3, it is best to be aware of your limits early so you won't waste time.

If you have already chosen a target school and it *is* more expensive, investigate that school's financial aid programs and present your parents with a comprehensive *written* list of options. Most schools offer work-study arrangements, special grants, loans, and some amount of federally subsidized aid. There are also numerous books available on financing a college education which provide information about state and federal aid, as well as obscure or specialized scholarships. Never assume you are not eligible for aid.

Various services exist that research scholarships and private sources of aid for you. The fee is usually $40 and if they don't find you $100 worth of aid, you get your money back. Be prepared, however, to spend a great deal of time filling out grant applications. Two other excellent resources are *Lovejoy's Guide to Financial Aid* (New York: Monarch Books, 1987), and *The A's and B's of Academic Scholarships* by Priscilla S. Goeller (Alexandria, VA: Octameron Press, 1988), which makes special note of scholarships available for transfer students.

FINANCIAL AID OPTIONS

- **Federal programs** include Pell Grants, Perkins Loans, College Work-Study Programs, Social Security Benefits for Children of Deceased or Disabled Parents, and Veterans Educational Benefits.[2] Call the **Federal Student Aid Information Center** 1-800-333-INFO, 9:00 a.m.–5:30 p.m., E.S.T., Monday–Friday.

- **State higher education agencies** each have their own aid programs with different award levels, eligibility criteria, and application procedures.

2. *The Student Guide: Financial Aid from the U.S. Department of Education—Grants, Loans and Work-Study,* 1989–90.

- Check **foundations,** religious organizations, fraternities or sororities, and town or city clubs. Include community and civic groups such as the American Legion, YMCA, Jaycees, and the Chamber of Commerce.

- **Companies,** as well as labor unions, have programs to help pay college costs for employees or members, or for their children.

- **Public libraries** have information on state and private sources of aid.

- **Scholarships** from the National Honor Society and National Merit Scholarships are available to students with high grades who qualify.

- **Veteran's Administration** offices may offer veteran's benefits.

- Investigate **organizations connected with your field of interest** (for example, the American Medical Association or the American Bar Association). These organizations are listed in the U.S. Department of Labor's *Occupational Outlook Handbook.*

Will My Financial Aid Transfer?

No. You will have to submit a new Financial Aid Form (FAF) and reapply for aid at your second school. But if you are currently receiving financial aid, you probably will qualify. Check to see if the school to which you are applying has need-blind admissions. Since many schools give scholarships based on ability as well as need, you may be eligible for even more money than you are getting now. The reverse is true, however, if you are currently on academic scholarship and your target school only gives aid based on need. It is important to get all the details about financial aid before you reapply.

Saving Without Aid

Even if you plan to transfer to a school with a higher tuition than your current one and you don't qualify for aid, it is possible that you could save money in the process. Examine carefully the expenses associated with both your present school and the one to which you want to transfer. Are you paying a lot to fly home every vacation? Is the cost of finding housing in the city sending you into debt? Would it be easier to get a part-time job if you had fewer academic requirements?

The following **Financial Breakdown** should help you get a better sense of your budget. Compare it with a breakdown of the college you might want to attend. Even if the tuition of your target school is more expensive, its location may save you some money. Moving from the North to a school closer to home and in a more temperate climate may cut your expenses down a good deal: on travel, heating (if you live off campus), and shipping of winter clothes. They may not make up the change in tuition, but if you present your parents with an itemized budget, these factors may help to compensate.

When dealing with money, and parents, it is important to show thought, consideration, and effort. Always give your parents a carefully *written* list of the reasons for which you want to transfer. If you know finances will be a major concern for your family, it is probably best to approach your parents after you have completed your research.

STRATEGIC FINANCIAL PLANNING

Transferring can also be used as a strategic option for cutting college costs. Many students enroll first at a less expensive school and then transfer to a more expensive one after their first or second year. Since the cost of one year at a junior or community college can be half as much as at a state university (and $16,000 less than at a private college), the plan of **Strategic Financial Planning** makes a lot of sense. Judith Margolin warns against this tactic, however, in *Financing a College Education: The Essential Guide for the 90's.* She argues that students who plan on transferring after two years "rarely accomplish the feat," and if they do, the process is delayed because of residency and credit requirements. Since it might take longer to graduate, the student may not save as much money as planned. Finally, she says that students who enroll in one school while planning to transfer to another are "living in limbo" and feel uncommitted to either college.[3]

These are legitimate concerns. A student who plans ahead, however, can avoid most, if not all, of these problems. First,

3. Judith Margolin, *Financing a College Education: The Essential Guide for the 90's* (New York: Plenum, 1989).

Financial Breakdown
for One Year

Tuition	$_____
Room	$_____
Board	$_____
Travel to and from school	$_____
Shipping expenses	$_____
Books & lab fees	$_____
Long-distance telephone bill	$_____
Average weekend travel for 1 month	$_____ × 7 mos = $_____
Average weekend expenses	$_____ × 30 wks = $_____
Average weekly expenses	$_____ × 30 wks = $_____

- -

TOTAL $_____

don't try to stay aloof from your first school. Get involved. Students who participate fully in the "collegiate experience" of junior colleges have a higher success rate for transferring.[4] Second, consider your various alternatives. If you choose to go

4. Arthur Cohen and Florence Brawer, *The Collegiate Function of Community Colleges* (San Francisco: Jossey-Bass, 1987).

to a two-year college, you will not have to worry about getting so attached to your school that you do not want to transfer. On the other hand, if you go to a four-year community or state college, you can always complete your education if for some reason you do not get accepted as a transfer student. Third, recognize that Strategic Financial Planning only works if you can get good grades at your initial school, so you can be sure of admission to your first-choice college when you want to transfer. Finally, do the necessary research for your second school before you even decide to enroll at the first one. Under no circumstances do you want to leave getting in to your target school to the last minute. Find out ahead of time about transfer credit, admissions criteria, and housing arrangements. Strategic Financial Planning is sure to backfire if you are not prepared in advance. Nevertheless, nearly half of all students who earn their associate degrees do transfer successfully to four-year institutions.

Of course, the greatest objection to Strategic Financial Planning is that many people do not want to spend two years at a "lesser" school. But as Martin Nemko writes in *How to Get an Ivy League Education at a State University,* a savvy student can get a first-class education practically anywhere:

> We've all been trained to believe that you get what you pay for. But with public colleges it's not true, because the government is picking up the tab. Nevertheless, I used to assume that private colleges had to be better. Otherwise, why would people spend all that money?
>
> Having surveyed over a thousand students and administrators from both public and private colleges, however, I've become very impressed with America's best public colleges. . . .
>
> I hope that this book will encourage students and their parents to think twice before spending the extra $40–50,000 on a private college.[5]

You may even find after two years that you are getting an excellent education where you are.

Michael Chin wasn't sure that he wanted to spend four years getting a college degree. So, having taken time off after high school, he enrolled at Hartnell Junior College, which he liked because it was small and close to home. "It was a cheap experiment to see if I wanted to go to college at all and invest that

5. Martin Nemko, *How to Get an Ivy League Education at a State University* (New York: Avon Books, 1988), p. ix.

kind of money." His parents were extremely supportive because Hartnell was practically free. He saved enough money in those two years to afford another two at the University of California at Santa Cruz. Michael said the transition was easy and that the junior college had prepared him well for university life. "I lived in a dorm with first-year students who had never had experience doing research or extensive writing, and a lot of them didn't really want to be there. They were just dying."

Going to a junior college first was not only financially advantageous for Michael, it provided excellent training for advanced study. Although he graduated 231 out of 285 in his high school class, Michael received his associate degree from Hartnell *magna cum laude.* Hartnell gave him the self-confidence and interest in learning necessary to do well at Santa Cruz.

Not everyone has the luxury of planning in advance. James Carson enrolled at Earlham University before he knew that he would have financial difficulties. Although he was on financial aid at Earlham, at the beginning of his sophomore year James inherited just enough money to lose his aid, but not enough to support himself fully. Rather than spending his entire savings on college, he decided to transfer to Indiana University. He wanted to stay at Earlham because of its strong Japanese Department, but, he said, "hopefully, when I get into upper-level courses I'll have the same challenging environment at I.U. as I have here."

As college costs continue to rise, more and more students are taking advantage of the transfer option. So, before you discount the possibility of attending your first-choice college because of finances, consider the alternatives. Two years at a junior or community college can provide a solid educational foundation at low cost. Remember, the only school on your diploma is the one you graduate from. Transferring may be a lot better than paying back loans for the rest of your life.

SAYING GOODBYE TO FRIENDS

"A lot of people I knew were thinking about leaving, but it made them uneasy that I was actually doing it."
—Eric Foster (Tufts to Columbia)

"My closest friends were also transferring, which made it a lot easier."
—Jason Hawkings (Fairleigh Dickinson to University of North Carolina)

"Some friends looked at me and said, 'You're lucky to get out of here.' I was really surprised."
—Sharon Patofosky (Lehigh to Hampshire)

"The hardest part about transferring was leaving my best friend."
—Karl Patrick (Georgia Tech to UVA)

"My friends were sad to see me go, but they knew how unhappy I was and that it was the right decision."
—Everybody

Your parents may present a host of objections to your decision to transfer, but they will never influence how you feel the way your friends will. Without question, the majority of transfers we talked to said they avoided telling their friends that they were planning to leave until the last possible minute. How do you look someone in the face whom you have just spent six months getting to know and say, "I'm miserable here"? And how do you explain your unhappiness? You certainly can't say, "I'm dissatisfied with the people I'm meeting."

On the other hand, probably the biggest reason most people choose not to leave is the fear of having to make new friends at another school. Ironically, as many college deans told us, transfers tend to be some of the most popular students at their new school and often take clear leadership roles. As long as you keep in touch, switching schools can greatly enhance your social life. After experiencing both LeMoyne and Boston College, Dawn Stimpson feels like she has "twice as many friends."

Saying goodbye, even if you hate the school, isn't easy. One student was shocked when his friends started accusing him of being a "malcontent." Friends tend to be loyal to their school and will resent the implication that it is less than perfect, so it is often hard for them to offer much-needed support. When talking to friends who are happy, it's best not to trash your school. Regardless of whether or not they agree with your criticisms, they will probably want to convince you to stay.

TRANSFERRING FOR LOVE

It is never easy to tell your friends that you are planning to leave. Especially if the friend is your lover. Eric Clark deliberately avoided dating anyone while at UCLA because he "didn't want to get involved in anything that would change my mind for the wrong reasons." If you do date, be honest about your future plans, and don't spend a lot of time talking about your misery.

What if you have already met the perfect person, and he or she is at another school? Janice Taylor left Washington University at St. Louis to join her boyfriend, Adam, at the University of Michigan. Her parents were appalled. They feared that she might get hurt. In the end, Janice married the man she transferred for. But she still advises those who are considering leaving for love not to change schools unless they have a number of other good reasons for transferring. Janice herself wanted to transfer to Michigan for a variety of reasons, and said she would have done so even if Adam had never been a student there.

What if they had broken up after she made the move? "If it's a large enough university, you can always start over," Janice said. Think about the future, which can be greatly affected by the size of your school. If you break up, will you still run into each other every day on the way to class? Will you be happy there without him or her?

The greatest advantage to transferring for a lover is that you avoid many of the ordinary hassles of readjustment. Apart from not having to worry about making friends, everything is easier if you know someone well at your new school. Picking classes, arranging housing, and learning your way around all become much simpler tasks.

Still, the risk of breaking up is great: is marriage really in your future? You cannot afford to think only in the short term. Moreover, you are likely to face great objection from your parents. If you can't find several other solid reasons to tell them you want to transfer, maybe it's really not a good idea at all. You can always look at distance as a true test of your relationship. On the other hand, as Janice said, "You might as well transfer and save yourself a fortune in phone bills."

Family, Friends, Finances, and Freud

This chapter was about resistance: who is not going to want you to transfer and why. We've tried to prepare you for your opposition and provide yet another opportunity for self-examination (transferring is a lot cheaper than psychoanalysis). By now, you should be absolutely sure about why you want to transfer. The only questions remaining are where, when, and how?

JESSICA WICKLER
New York University–University of Houston–George Mason

"My mother wasn't exactly thrilled when I told her that I had to change schools to be with John." Jessica's desire to transfer for love was not the only reason her mother was concerned. Jessica had already transferred. After one year she had left NYU to attend the University of Houston. Wanting to join her boyfriend in Washington, D.C., she hoped to transfer yet again, this time to George Mason.

From the beginning, Jessica knew that she might not be able to afford four years at NYU. *"But I wanted to study art history and I had this idea of what New York would be. I saw it as an adventure."* Manhattan lived up to her expectations, and she took full advantage of life outside of the university. Working at the Rich Perlow Gallery was *"a terrific opportunity"* to use what she was learning about art at school. But although the academics at NYU were excellent, the cramped dorm life and lack of privacy were difficult to get used to. By the end of her first year Jessica was feeling ready to leave.

Getting turned down for financial aid sealed the decision. Her parents had recently divorced and because of *"very complicated rules about tax returns,"* she didn't meet eligibility requirements. There was no other way for her family to cover the $15,000 a year it cost to go to NYU. So Jessica returned to Texas. *"Even though I loved New York, leaving was pretty easy. I wasn't particularly attached to NYU and Houston was home."*

Jessica describes her sophomore year at the University of Houston as *"comfortable."* She lived off campus with a friend from high school and socialized with people she knew from the city's art community. After her first semester Jessica realized that *"writing came more naturally than art* history," so she switched majors. The English Literature Department was strong and she did very well academically. Although she enjoyed her time at the University of Houston, "no one was surprised that I only stayed a year."

Jessica met John at a party that a friend made her go to. "I fell pretty much instantly in love." They were inseparable for six months. Then John decided to move to Washington, D.C., because he wasn't making enough money as a forester in Texas. Jessica took a large risk and decided to move with him. "I completely jumped into it. I didn't really think about what it meant." She was ready to move on, and this seemed like the perfect opportunity.

During the summer, Jessica applied to three schools in Washington, D.C. She was accepted in early August and chose George Mason for its strong creative writing program. Jessica's grandparents had been paying for her education since she left NYU. "They offered, and it was the easiest way to handle things." So, even though George Mason was more expensive than University of Houston, she could still afford to go. In her transfer essay, she stressed that this would be her last change. "I wanted to give them the impression that I was ready to settle down and work diligently toward graduating."

The down side of all this moving around was the difficulty of arranging transfer credit. Since each of the three schools' academic requirements were slightly different, Jessica had to repeat various classes. She never took summer school but will have to spend an extra semester at George Mason making up credit. She should complete her degree in four and a half years. Her primary advice to other transfer students is to be aggressive. "Get to know the system, because the school isn't going to take care of everything."

Jessica's life at George Mason is very different from what it was at her two prior universities. She has found excellent professors but few close friends at school. Her work and social life no longer revolve around the campus. She lives with John in the suburb of Arlington and commutes to school. "Sometimes the distance is hard. I've given up the sense of being part of a school." But she also feels that she already "did the college experience." She likes living in Washington and plans to teach high school English after graduating.

Jessica took a large risk transferring in order to sustain a relationship. Almost anyone would have counseled her against it. Looking back, she admits that "life would have been a lot easier had I stayed in one school for four years." But the romance has lasted, and Jessica is very happy with her decision.

Chapter 3

If Only I Knew Then What I Know Now

THE SIX-STEP PLAN TO SUCCESSFULLY CHANGING SCHOOLS

BREAKING UP
Reevaluation

TELLING THE FOLKS
Renegotiation

PLAYING THE FIELD
Research

MAKING THE FIRST MOVE
Reapplication

WRITING THE LOVE LETTER
Revision

STARTING OVER
Readjustment

*First I lay down in Papa Bear's great big
bed. But that was too hard. Then I lay down
in Mama Bear's medium-sized bed. But that
was too soft. Then I lay down in Baby Bear's
wee tiny bed.*
And that was just right.

—Goldilocks

When applying to college the second time around, you have a
clear advantage over high school students: you know what
college is about. You are no longer a wide-eyed senior blissfully
fantasizing about collegiate life. Living in dorms, sitting
through introductory classes, and eating in dining halls has
given you perspective. And perspective is invaluable as a
transfer applicant because you can no longer afford to make any
mistakes. Nobody wants to transfer twice.

THIS ISN'T HIGH SCHOOL ANYMORE

One or two years of perspective has probably shown you that
the traditional approach to applying to college makes little
sense. Most of us were taught to apply the same way: to two or
three schools that we were fairly sure we could get into, to one
or two schools that seemed like a challenge, and to one or two
schools that had to accept us, just in case we didn't get in
anywhere else. So the average student applied to somewhere
between four and seven schools, hoping desperately to get into
his or her "first choice."

We call this approach the "reach or fall" plan, that is, if
you're lucky, then you will reach the school at the top of your
list, and if you're not, you will fall into the school at the bottom.
The problem with this plan, as you already know, is that there
is nothing safe about falling into a school where you would be
miserable. And there is nothing so great about reaching a
school where you would be academically out of place.

The second problem with the "reach or fall" plan is that after
filling out six or seven applications, visiting six or seven
colleges, and having interviews at six or seven colleges, who has
the time to do anything else? *But the biggest problem of all with
the "reach or fall" plan is that the time and effort you spend
reaching for a school too high inevitably causes you to fall into
one too low.*

GETTING IT *JUST RIGHT*

You have probably realized that it makes much more sense to find a school that is *just right* for you and to concentrate all of your time, energy, and effort on getting into that one *just right* school. Choosing only one target school allows you to get to know it intimately and thoroughly. Which will:

- Improve your essay

- Strengthen your overall application

- Heighten your performance in an admissions interview

- Make readjustment easier

Most important, if you know the target school well, you can be sure it is the best school for you. In high school they said, "If you don't like it, you can always transfer." But they didn't mean twice.

PLAYING THE FIELD
Researching Schools

Finding a school that is just right for you and getting to know that school are complex tasks; they take research. But since you have already spent a year or two in higher education, you know enough about college life to make researching easy. You know who to talk to, what questions to ask, and what books to read. Whereas high school seniors tend to have vague, unrealistic expectations about college, you should have clear goals and a more pragmatic sense of university life. With the perspective of a college education, you are miles ahead of someone applying for the first time.

The trick is making use of that perspective, which is what the rest of this chapter is about, because it is easy to forget what you already know, or feel ashamed to ask what you don't.

What if you can't find a target school that is just right? Well, there are over 1,500 accredited four-year colleges in the United States (275 of which Edward Fiske of *The New York Times* calls "selective"), 1,211 junior (two-year) colleges, and many thousands of universities abroad. If you can't find the right school (or one even close), maybe you should reconsider if college itself is right for you.

You may very well be leery of advice that says apply only to one school, especially when every guidebook, guidance counselor, parent, and friend is telling you otherwise. What if your ideal target school is simply too hard to get into? Read on and we think you will see how research can help you get into even the most selective schools.

The foundation of academic scholarship is research, so if you demonstrate excellent research abilities in your admissions search, you can prove that you have the skills to succeed in college.

Secondary Sources

The first question is where to begin. With so many schools out there and so little time to choose, you must narrow down your choices as quickly as possible. Researching a target school is just like researching a paper. There are two places to look for information: primary sources and secondary sources. When you begin, you will want to utilize as many secondary sources as possible.

Secondary sources include college guidebooks, newspaper and magazine articles, guidance counselors, and any other source not directly related to the school. The appendix at the end of the book provides vital transfer information on over one hundred colleges and universities. Each profile includes information regarding tuition, housing, financial aid, articulation agreements, residency requirements, admissions criteria, and cites the number of transfers who apply annually and the number who are admitted.

The best secondary resource available is the *Fiske Guide to Colleges* (New York: Time Books, 1990). It is the definitive guide with nearly three hundred in-depth profiles. Rather than being a mere list of statistics, the book provides a strong sense of the character of each college. Both students and administrators completed extensive questionnaires about the academics, social life, and general quality of life at their school. Their candid opinions and perceptions portray both the strengths and weaknesses of each institution. The *Fiske Guide to Colleges* is an invaluable tool for finding the college that is just right for you.

In addition, *Barron's Profiles of American Colleges* (New York: Barron's Educational Series, 1989) contains very basic transfer information (deadlines, residency requirement) for over 1,500 schools. And Martin Nemko's *How to Get an Ivy League Education at a State University* (New York: Avon Books, 1988) provides good information about state schools.

Before you continue in your search, make a list of specific characteristics that you expect to find in an ideal school. Make sure that these are qualities you really care about, so that you can afford to be inflexible about them later.

**Ten things that must be true
of your target school:**

_____

- -

- -

- -

- -

- -

- -

- -

- -

- -

_____

OTHER CONSIDERATIONS—ROTC

Well over 800 colleges and universities participate in the Reserved Officers Training Corps programs. Although it is not common practice, ROTC students do transfer. You cannot switch programs, going from Army to Navy, for instance, but you can switch schools. The process is slightly more complicated, and there are several steps you must follow before you even apply.

The contract you initially signed to join ROTC specifies your college, academic major, and date of graduation. You cannot change any of those terms without getting Headquarters approval or you will be in breach of contract. As Commander Dugen of the Pentagon said, "In a sense, ROTC students are government property."

Approval to transfer is decided on a case-by-case basis and cost is an important factor. The majority of ROTC scholarships pay full college tuition, textbooks, and a monthly allowance. So, if you're transferring to an equally or less expensive school, there should be no problem. Difficulties arise when switching schools involves a significant financial increase. If you are prepared to pay the difference, state that clearly when you apply for permission. Generally, the military wants to keep its cadets and is willing to cover expenses.

Another issue to consider is whether or not your target school offers your ROTC program. If not, you may sign up at a cross town unit. It's a good idea to call and ask to talk to students in that program. Commuting changes the experience and you may prefer to stay where you are.

Since the ROTC curriculum is standardized, you should have no trouble switching units. However, the amount of academic credit given toward a degree for ROTC work varies from school to school. Make sure you find out about your target college's credit policies early.

If you are not currently enrolled in an ROTC unit and would like to join after transferring, two-year programs do exist that are primarily available to transfer students and veterans. To enroll in the two-year Professional Officer Course, you must apply in your sophomore year. The major difference between the programs is your service obligation. Contact a recruiting officer at the school to which you are applying for more information.

The Personals

Once you have narrowed your search down to three or four schools, you can begin the challenging task of finding the right one. Flipping through college guidebooks is like reading the Personals—all you get is general, brief, and usually glowing descriptions. If you are to find anything close to the school of your dreams, you are going to have to "date" each one.

Since college is going to be a two- or three-year relationship, you can't afford to get involved without meeting. "The biggest mistake I made the first time was not visiting," said Denise Harding, who saw Roger Williams for the first time the day she arrived for orientation. She stayed only one semester. When she reapplied as a transfer, Denise made sure she saw every campus. It is imperative that you visit a school before you apply to transfer. Make sure you have done as much preliminary research as possible to get the most out of your trip.

Preparing for Your First Date: Primary Sources

Before you meet your school "in person," you should prepare by consulting as many **primary sources** as possible. A written primary source is anything published by the school, including school newspapers, magazines, alumni publications, academic journals, and admissions brochures. You can send away for each of these sources by mail. They will give you invaluable insight about the day-to-day life of the school. Most important, get a copy of the course catalogue to examine the curriculum and see if the courses, departments, and available majors interest you.

People can also serve as primary sources and will give you a very different perspective from the college brochure. Talk to alumni and friends who are currently enrolled. You may want to find out if any instructors at your present college attended your target school as undergraduates. They will be particularly helpful, especially if you can get them to write you recommendations later.

The most useful primary source is a professor at the school you want to attend. One dean of admissions suggests writing to professors in your department and including photocopies of all correspondence in your application. The letters will prove that you are highly motivated as well as demonstrate your interest in the school and in your subject. Even a single letter can make a big difference: admissions committees give considerable weight to faculty opinions.

Sample Letter to a Professor

Glen Heller
Box 5137
University of North Carolina
Chapel Hill, NC 27514

Dr. Linda Alcoff
Department of Philosophy
Syracuse University
Syracuse, NY 13244

Dear Professor Alcoff,

After reading your article "Cultural Feminism and Post Structuralism" last month in *Signs,* I became fascinated with the ideas of Foucault. Although I am a philosophy major at the University of North Carolina, I have never studied contemporary French theorists. I would be interested in reading any further books or articles you might recommend on the subject.

I would also appreciate it if you could send me any information about your department, as I may be transferring to Syracuse next year. I am most interested in studying European philosophy; is that a strong area of your department?

I look forward to hearing from you and to reading more of your work. Thank you.

Sincerely,

Glen Heller

VISITING—THE FIRST DATE

On a first date you are always trying to figure out whether or not you are compatible. Does this relationship have a future? Do I want to invest a lot more time, money, and emotional commitment? The only way to find out the answers is to make conversation, and good conversation begins with asking the right questions.

In most cases, your first visit to the campus will last no more than twenty-four hours. So you need a systematic approach to collecting information. On the next page is a list of people to talk to and questions to ask them. Note that all the questions are very specific. You can always find more general information in secondary sources. The purpose of visiting is to obtain knowledge you cannot get otherwise. Remember that the more prepared you are beforehand, the more useful an interview will be. Also, ask for students' names and phone numbers so that you can get in touch with them later. Your first few weeks as a transfer student won't seem so lonely if you already know a few people on campus.

During your visit you will also want to sit in on classes, eat in the dining hall, and check out the dorms. Before you measure the quality of the school by a class you visit, however, find out what the reputation of that class is on campus. Use everything you already know about college life to find information. You are well aware that classes on a campus range from the incredible to the unmentionable, so don't judge a school by one bad lecture. On the other hand, if everyone you talk to says that the course you visited is supposed to be one of the best on campus, then you have something by which to judge. Even better than relying on popular opinion, talk to the professor after class.

Many people are embarrassed to seek out faculty members or administrators. "Why would they have time to talk to me?", you wonder. They have time because faculty and administrators care about who comes to their school. Athletes, for example, usually establish a solid rapport with coaches before attending a school. The coach becomes the athlete's advocate during the admissions process and after the student arrives on campus.

Any dean or faculty member you speak with *may* tell the admissions office of your interest in the school. Harvard's

People you absolutely must talk with to find out if a school is right for you:

- Several presently enrolled students
- Several presently enrolled transfer students, one of whom, if possible, transferred from the school which you are currently attending (ask admissions office for names and numbers)
- One faculty member in your department

People you really should talk with if you want to make sure that this is the right school for you and if you want to improve your chances of getting in:

- Several faculty in your department
- Students taking part in the extracurricular (or political) activities you are most interested in
- A coach of any team on which you plan to play

People who are surprisingly helpful if you are truly serious about the researching process:

- Deans and student advisors
- Administrative assistants
- Alumni

transfer coordinator recommends asking professors to contact the admissions committee on your behalf. Do so, however, only if you made a very good impression. This requires asking well-prepared questions. Although the questions we include below will provide you with important information about the school, it is vital to show professors your *intellectual* interest in their subjects. Therefore, it is better to speak to faculty in your department than in a random one, so that you have something of substance to discuss. You also want to learn as much about your department as you can before you decide if this is where you want to spend two or three years.

Questions To Ask

To the Students

- Do professors teach most classes or do they rely on teaching assistants?
- Do lecture classes usually have smaller sections?
- What is the grading system?
- Are professors required to hold office hours?
- Is getting shut out of classes a problem?
- Is it difficult to get into seminars or upper-level courses?
- Who are the good professors in your department?

- What is the best housing on campus?
- What is the worst housing on campus?
- How much is housing?
- Is the campus safe?
- Are buildings accessible to disabled students?

- How is dating?
- Do most people go away on weekends?
- Do people go to dances/forums/theater on campus?
- Is entertainment expensive?
- Are there cheap restaurants within walking distance?
- How important is the Greek system?
- Are there off-campus parties?
- What is the drinking age, and is it enforced by the school?
- Are drugs used frequently?

- How are race relations?
- Is there a large African American/Asian/Hispanic community?
- How are gays and lesbians treated?
- Are there minority support groups?

- Are publications/theater groups/athletics respected?

To the Professors

- Are students interested/informed/ambitious/competitive?
- How often do you hold office hours?
- How large is your average class?

- How large is the average class in the department?
- How much emphasis is placed on teaching versus research?
- Does the school offer academic resources such as tutors/ writing centers?
- Are students required to write a thesis?

If you sat in on his/her class:

- How was this class compared to other classes you teach?
- Do students participate regularly?

To the Administrators

- Do deans hold office hours?
- What counseling services are available to students?
- What is the advising system—are students assigned advisors or do they select their own?
- Does the school have an ROTC program?
- What are the policies regarding cross registration with other schools?

To the Alumni

- Was the school helpful in career placement?
- Have school connections been valuable?
- Do you feel the school prepared you well?
- Would you go there again?
- Are you still active in alumni organizations, do you give money?

Contacting the admissions office before you actually apply is one of the most important steps in the research process. Ask directly about your honest chances of admission. Harvard, for example, will not consider an applicant whom they feel does not have enough transferable credits to graduate in the usual four years. Save yourself time by finding out if it is possible for you to get in before you go to the effort of applying.

Admissions Officer (after checking in the Appendix)

- How is transfer credit arranged?
- Will my courses transfer?
- How many students apply to transfer annually?
- How many are admitted?
- What are the minimum requirements for admission?

- Are SAT or ACT scores required?
- What are the average credentials of an admitted transfer student?
- Do you give preference to any types of transfers?
- What is the housing situation for transfer students?
- What are the deadlines for admission?
- Is an interview required? If not, is one granted for transfer applicants?
- Is financial aid available for transfer students?
- What is the residency requirement?
- Are transfer students allowed to study abroad?

Not all of these questions may be relevant to your needs, but they demonstrate how specific a good question must be. The more specific the question, however, the more you will have to extrapolate from the answers you receive. For example, if two or three alumni tell you that they still give money each year, you can deduce that they enjoyed their undergraduate experience and feel pride in their school. Still, avoid jumping to conclusions from too little information. One student may tell you that all classes are huge lectures, but that may be just because he or she is an Economics major. The more people you talk to, the more accurate your knowledge of the target school will be.

You may also have personal interests that are not fully represented here. For instance, minority students need to ask different questions when researching. *The Black Student's Guide to the Colleges* by Barry Beckham (Providence, RI: Beckham House, 1984) provides descriptions of black student life at over 150 schools, as well as information on scholarships. As Beckham says in the Introduction: "Black students, particularly on white campuses, are concerned about their psychological as well as academic survival. The general climate, the social life, and the kinds of organizations that relate to their own cultural background are matters central to black students' emotional well-being."

The questions that we have listed are all supposed to help you answer two larger issues: Will you be happy at the school *as a transfer?* And how do you get in?

Will You Be Happy as a Transfer at This School?

If you played the "reach or fall" game the first time you applied to college, you may now be trying to climb out of the hole you fell into. Before you continue to reach for that first-choice school, however, watch out. Assuming you searched well in high school, what was once your first-choice college may have been ideal. But the perfect school for a first-year student is often not so great for a transfer. For example, start looking now for a school that makes readjustment as painless as possible. Does your ideal school offer a transfer orientation program? Is this program specifically designed for transfers, or are they clumped together with first-year students? Are transfers guaranteed housing, or are they put at the bottom of the list?

At the University of Michigan, transfers are isolated on North Campus, fifteen minutes away from the main university and only accessible by bus. As Daphne Hero said, "It doesn't give you a very good first impression of the school." Daphne tried desperately to change her housing, but to no avail. The situation can be even worse for transfers at NYU and Columbia. They are not guaranteed campus housing and therefore must contend with Manhattan landlords, and rents, on their own.

Call the admissions office of any school to which you are serious about applying and ask for the names of several transfer students whom you can talk to. Definitely speak with the transfer coordinator about reorientation and housing. If your target school doesn't have a transfer coordinator, or is unhelpful, that may reflect the priorities of the institution. Also find out about other counseling programs available to students. Although you might never have needed an advisor at your present school, you will certainly want easy-to-find guidance during readjustment.

If you have hopes of going away for a semester, find out about leavetaking policies for transfer students. Many schools restrict transfers from taking semesters abroad as part of their residency requirement (see Chapter 4).

Finally, think about transfer credit. Meagan Strompson found out in July that Hampshire would not accept any of her credits from Smith. Hampshire operates on a completely different system from other schools and will not grant credit for work done elsewhere. Most students are not prepared to give up an entire year. Find out about general transfer credit policies before you apply.

- Get names and phone numbers of transfer students
- Talk to the transfer coordinator
- Ask about housing

- Investigate orientation programs
- Research residency requirements and time off

How Do You Get In?

Research is ultimately valuable only if it helps you get admitted to your target school. Your job is to find out as much about your target school's admissions policies as possible. What counts most in the application? What are they looking for in the essay?

Laurie Robinson, who recently graduated from Nassau Community College, told us that she did not apply to any private schools because she did not feel she had strong enough credentials or the financial resources. Little did she know that both Amherst and Williams, two highly selective private colleges, give preference for "nontraditional" applicants, meaning graduates of community colleges. The assistant director of admissions at Williams said that the school is "looking for students who would add significantly to the diversity of the class." Moreover, both schools have need-blind financial aid policies.

If you think you are a disadvantaged applicant, use your research to help you make the most of your special trait. The state of California has just pumped millions of dollars into the University of California system in order to help minority transfer students: African Americans, Native Americans, Mexican Americans, and Latin Americans. Information like this can help save you countless hours in the final admissions process.

Remember that schools accept transfers for a variety of reasons, including the need to fill undersubscribed departments. Make sure you know what students your target school is looking for. If you haven't decided on a major but you are interested in the sciences, you may temporarily want to declare Geochemistry. Don't ever tell an admissions officer, however, that you are interested in a subject in which you clearly are not; such a plan can only backfire. In all probability, there is *something* about you that makes you attractive to the school (if nothing else, your overwhelming desire to go there). The more you know about a college, the better your chances of finding out why they need you.

Nevertheless, as you continue your research, you may discover that getting in to your target school would be practically impossible. We met one Harvard student who applied twice to transfer to the University of California at Santa Cruz. She was denied admission both times. We were shocked. From Harvard? So we called the admissions office at Santa Cruz and found out that first priority is always given to California community college students. This past year, UCSC received applications from students at Harvard, Princeton, and Yale, and they were forced to reject them all because of the overwhelming number of community college applicants. One phone call could have saved our friend a good deal of time, effort, and $50 in application fees.

VIDEO DATING

Obviously if you're transferring to the University of Alaska from Emory, you may not be able to visit. But recognize that you are taking a very large risk. There is another way, however. Many colleges now produce video advertisements as part of their marketing strategy. Your old high school may have such videos on file. Or you could go to a local public school and ask a guidance counselor to order the tape you wish to see. You won't get a full picture of the school from its video (you'll never see the really ugly dorms hidden behind the athletic center, for example), but it's better than nothing at all. Still, we recommend visiting at all costs, or choosing a school closer to home.

If your ideal school has admissions criteria way above your academic record . . . Or if you don't want to put all of your eggs in one basket . . .

Go back to your preliminary research and find one or two target schools that are as close as possible to your ideal school. Use the list of **Ten things that must be true of your target school** (on p. 51) and pick one or two schools that have as many of those characteristics as possible, but are *slightly* easier to get into. The difference between this school and a "safety" in the traditional sense is that you would be extremely happy to attend this institution, and the admissions criteria are not so far below your own record that you would feel academically out of place.

If you decide to apply to more than one school, then you are going to have to make a choice. Either you will have to divide the time spent researching between the various schools, or you are going to have to spend double, or triple, or quadruple the amount of time doing the research. (Also keep in mind that if you send your SAT scores to more than one college, each receives a list of all the other colleges to which you have sent your scores. Any college that doubts whether or not you will actually matriculate if admitted may not bother to accept you in the first place.)

Whichever approach you choose, keep in mind that your chances of getting accepted are proportional to how well you know the school.

MELANIE PANKO
Wheelock College–Boston College

For Melanie Panko, transferring was a breeze. She actively planned ahead, enrolled her parents' support, searched intensively for a new school, and handled transfer credit well ahead of time.

After two months at Wheelock College, Melanie started preparing to transfer. Wheelock is a small all-female college in Boston, known for its Education and Social Work departments. Melanie had applied to Wheelock's "early decision" program and was planning to pursue a career in teaching. At the time, she was sure that she wanted a college with "a specialized focus." But after a miserable first semester, she realized that "Wheelock was giving me professional training instead of an education." Melanie found out how small the school really was when she couldn't minor in English because the department "only had seven courses."

Wanting to stay in the area, Melanie immediately narrowed her search to only Boston schools. She wanted a solid liberal arts college with strong Education and English departments as well as a co-educational environment. Melanie started researching by reading all the college guidebooks over again. She reconsidered all the schools she had looked at originally. Even though it seemed like repeating senior year in high school, Melanie was planning to apply to only one school. "You don't need to do that college thing over again—eight schools and all is too much."

Her parents were very supportive of Melanie's decision to transfer because they knew she was miserable. Plus they knew she was "bored there, and certainly not learning enough to be paying $20,000." Despite the lack of challenge, Melanie worked hard academically. She knew good grades

*were a vital part of the transfer admissions process. Melanie
left Wheelock with a 4.0 GPA.*

*She was very familiar with Boston College because she
had spent "a lot of time there socially." After she gained a
good sense of the school from its students, she started
interviewing B.C. faculty. She describes the meetings as
"good, but weird, because I didn't know exactly what I
wanted them to tell me. Mostly they told me about the
philosophy of the Education Department and distribution
requirements."*

*In her official interview with the admissions office,
Melanie asked "very pointed questions." She was well
prepared and made sure to bring up the issue of transfer
credit. "They were impressed by my knowledge."*

*Her second semester at Wheelock, Melanie chose her
classes with "both catalogues side by side." She tried to
match course descriptions and fulfill, ahead of time, some of
B.C.'s extensive requirements. "I was prepared to fight for
my courses and have professors write letters. I really didn't
want to lose a semester." Her planning paid off and all of
Melanie's credits transferred.*

*Even so, Melanie doesn't have the freedom to take any
courses she wants. She still has several major requirements
to fulfill and her biggest concern is "getting two years of a
foreign language under my belt." Wheelock did not offer
languages and B.C. requires proficiency in order to
graduate. Although Melanie has more than enough credits,
she is still two courses behind. She doesn't mind the
thought of summer school as long as she "didn't lose
anything from Wheelock."*

*Regardless of her preparation, adjusting to the school's
social life was still difficult. "B.C. is very cliquish. And
since I lived in the mandatory quiet dorm, I didn't get to
meet people that way." Melanie purposely stayed away from
extracurricular activities to make adjusting easier. "I just
wanted to get my bearings."*

*Another adjustment was going from the intimacy of a
small college to the red tape of a large university.
"Professors aren't always willing to talk to you and I had to
get used to that." Nevertheless, Melanie is "a billion times
happier" than she was at Wheelock.*

*After spending a full year in the School of Education,
Melanie transferred again: this time internally, to B.C.'s
School of English. Even though intracampus transferring is
an easier process, Melanie still had to choose her courses
carefully. Since each school has its own requirements the
transition between departments can often be difficult.*

Melanie made sure that all of her second-semester courses corresponded with English requirements. "I had been wavering between English and Education for a while, so I took lots of courses in both."

The application procedure was informal, and the most important factor was an interview with the head of the English Department. After looking at her record, she told Melanie, "You're more organized than the English majors who were here to begin with."

The transfer went smoothly and Melanie is pleased with both changes. She advises other transfer students to think seriously about the decision. "Because you don't make the decision lightly, you really need to research carefully."

Chapter 4

Getting Out
(and In Again)

THE SIX-STEP PLAN TO SUCCESSFULLY CHANGING SCHOOLS

BREAKING UP
Reevaluation

TELLING THE FOLKS
Renegotiation

PLAYING THE FIELD
Research

MAKING THE FIRST MOVE
Reapplication

WRITING THE LOVE LETTER
Revision

STARTING OVER
Readjustment

*I absolutely cannot see how one can later
make up for having failed to go to a good
school at the right time.*
            —*Nietzsche*, Will to Power

You've decided to leave, told your folks, and carefully researched your target school. Now it's time to make the first move.

You can obtain a transfer application by writing or calling the admissions office. The application is similar to the form for high school students, but contains certain sections that are quite different, including the essay question and the recommendations. Each aspect of the reapplication process is described below. Pay careful attention to the information regarding transfer credit.

REAPPLICATION
Timing Is Everything

*"Transferring after one year is a really bad
idea. You just can't judge a school by
freshman year. Wait, and things may be a
lot better as a sophomore."* (Half the people
we interviewed)

*"If there's any advice I have, it's don't wait.
Get out as soon as possible. If you hate
school, there's no reason to go back for a
second year of hell."* (The other half)

Choosing when to reapply can almost be as hard as deciding whether or not to transfer at all. But most people who have transferred are adamant about when is the best time.

There are several reasons why it is better to apply before sophomore year. You will have more time to get settled in your new school and more time to make friends once you arrive. Reapplying after one year also gives you the opportunity to apply again just in case you get denied the first time. Finally, you won't experience the difficulty of leaving friends with whom you have spent two years.

Yet, there are many other reasons why it is better to wait two full years. Your transcript will be more complete. You will be more certain that transferring is the right decision and that your unhappiness is due to intrinsic incompatibility rather than superficial discontent. And lastly, two years of college should prepare you better for both research and reapplication.

So, when *is* the best time to apply?

Ask your target school. Many colleges prefer to accept transfers after one year. Others need to see two years of college-level work in order to accurately judge a student's performance. Some schools have flexible residency requirements and accept transfers for all classes. Find out if your school has a preference, and take advantage of that fact.

Residency

Regardless of when you transfer, you need to be aware of **residency requirements.** Every school requires that a student complete a minimum amount of work "in residence," i.e., paying tuition. The residency requirement is usually measured either in credit hours or in semesters. You may have already completed as many hours or semesters as allowed out of residence. If so, you should not wait to transfer or you might have to spend more than four years in college.

Converting credit hours can be tricky, however, because some schools only count *transferable credits.* For example, you have earned 60 credits at your first school when you apply to transfer, but your second school will only accept 30 of those credits toward your degree. If the residence requirement is 60 credits (4 sems.), then the maximum number of credits allowed out of residence is also 60, so you could wait until you have earned another 2 semesters of credit (30 units) if you wanted to. For a full discussion of transferability, see **Transfer Credit** below.

Mid-Year Admission

Another point to consider while trying to decide when to transfer is **mid-year application.** Most schools accept transfer students for the spring, as well as the fall, semester. In fact, schools generally accept many more for one of the two semesters, so you may want to find out when your target school accepts the highest percentage of transfers. Some colleges have only one application date but defer admission for a number of students to the spring semester. (If you are deferred and don't know what to do for the first semester, see Chapter 6 for information about taking time off.)

Transferring mid-year has its own advantages and disadvantages. Some people feel that adjustment is more difficult in the middle of the year. Others recommend a mid-year transition because schools tend to offer second-semester orientation programs designed especially for transfer students. Generally, fall transfers are placed in the orientation program for first-year students. If you are considering applying mid-year, make sure your school does offer some sort of reorientation for transfers.

Reapplying During the First Year

Although transferring mid-year is a useful opportunity, we caution against reapplying after just one semester. Three months of college is usually not enough time for you to judge a school. Nor is it enough time for a new school to judge you. If you do want to change schools immediately, you will probably have to apply as a **first-year applicant,** in which case you will not receive any transfer credit. This is a useful alternative if you are doing poorly academically because you will not have to send your college transcript. It may, however, not be an option. Some colleges, such as those in the City University of New York (CUNY) system, regard a student who has been enrolled in college for any length of time as a transfer applicant.

Déjà Vu

Although reapplying may seem like senior year all over again, it isn't. Don't be deceived by the apparent similarity of the processes: everything from the interview to the essay is different the second time around. Schools are looking for particular qualities in transfer students, so getting out, and in again, requires new strategies.

There is an important contrast between the way colleges judge transfer students and the way they judge high school applicants. High school students are selected on the *probability* of their future success in college. High school transcripts are analyzed, but since these do not reflect college-level work they are not the sole criteria for admission. Admissions officers consider many additional factors, such as standardized tests, extracurricular accomplishments, and community service.

When officers review a transfer student's application,

however, they don't have to take these other factors into consideration. The college record is proof of how well the applicant can handle college-level work. *The most important part of the transfer application, therefore, is the college transcript.*

THE TRANSFER PARADOX

If you don't have good grades, it's practically impossible to transfer. But if you're miserable, it's practically impossible to get good grades.

CREATING A TRANSFER'S TRANSCRIPT

But, remember, reapplying is different from applying the first time. And the college transcript is different from the high school one. While a college admissions officer will examine closely and often call a high school to determine the true performance of a student, *good grades on a college transcript are good grades;* an admissions officer can only guess at the difficulty of your classes.

Ideally, college should be about intellectual exploration, but as a transfer student you have to be grade-conscious. This does not mean that you should take only "gut" classes, but you must be strategic when planning your schedule. Most colleges and universities claim to check the level of all transfer applicants' courses. And though some, like Fordham, have an extensive library of school catalogues, determining the depth of a class is not as easy as it sounds. Reading a brief description in a course catalogue reveals nothing about the professor's standards, the student's flair for the subject, or the level of the grading. The ease or difficulty of a course is highly subjective, which is to your advantage. The following tips (in addition to studying) should help improve your college record:

- Always take classes that you find interesting
- Avoid your weak subjects (postpone them if they are required)
- Find intellectually stimulating courses that are graded easily

- Don't take courses from professors with reputations for tough grading
- Balance your schedule so that you are doing different types of work (reading, writing, lab work, drawing)
- Don't take Pass/Fail classes
- Stay away from classes with superficial names like "Fashion Merchandising" or "Sport in American Society"

In general, colleges want to see that you have taken solid courses that will fit into *their* curriculum. Some schools even determine the viability of an applicant by whether or not his or her classes will transfer. No school wants to admit a student who must start over from scratch. Remember, your transcript counts most. So get good grades.

WHAT IF IT'S TOO LATE?

Unfortunately, many students decide they want to transfer after a year or two of getting bad grades. But by taking advantage of each step of the reapplication process, you can still get admitted even if your transcript is mediocre.

The interview, recommendations, the application forms, and most of all the essay give you the opportunity to prove that you will do well as a transfer and that your reason for wanting to transfer is valid. From the standpoint of an admissions officer, the most—sometimes the only—valid reasons are academic. So, even if you are depressed because your school is in the middle of nowhere, you will have a much better chance of getting admitted if you can demonstrate an *academic* reason for transferring.

REASON FOR LEAVING VS. REASON FOR APPLYING

In Chapter 1, you clarified your reasons for leaving. They can range from boredom with the social scene to distress about the weather. But those reasons may not satisfy an admissions officer, nor explain why you have chosen the school you want to transfer *to*. There are probably a hundred schools with both more parties and better weather. Admissions officers want to know why you are applying to their school.

As we have said, a reason for applying is only valid if it is academic: you want to study with a particular professor, enroll in a special program, or make use of rare facilities. For example, if you wish to go to Columbia, you must convince the admissions office that it is the ideal college for you, ideal because it offers an academic environment missing at your present school. It is not enough to say that you dream of attending Columbia because it is in New York City, since Pace, Hunter, Manhattan College, NYU, and Fordham are all in New York as well.

Using what you have learned from your research, you should be able to find several good reasons for applying, even if they were not what initially attracted you to the school. For example, you are satisfied as a Biology major at your present school but you want to leave to be with your girlfriend at another college. Unfortunately, the admissions committee won't be moved by your devotion. But during your research you discover that your girlfriend's school offers marine biology, a subject you've always wanted to study. Then your reason for leaving is love and your reason for applying is curricular.

What if you can't find anything about the school that would qualify as a good reason for applying? Keep in mind that academic reasons for applying are numerous and varied. A better department, a particular professor, larger classes, smaller classes, more challenging upper-level classes, better resources, or a different focus in the curriculum are all solid reasons for applying.

Although some reasons for applying may be valid, they may not be *compelling*. For instance, you state on your application that you want to transfer to Duke because its English Department has a strong reputation. But since so many schools have good English programs, that is not compelling enough to persuade an admissions committee. You will have a much better chance of acceptance if you can say, honestly, that you want to study Marxist literary criticism with Professor Frederic Jameson. In other words, the more specific your reasons for applying, the more compelling they will be. And the better your research, the better your chances of getting in.

A reason for applying is *valid* if it is academic and honest. It is *compelling* if it is specific, particular to that school, and shows why you are dissatisfied with your present educational milieu. In order to communicate your valid and compelling reasons for applying to the admissions committee, you will first have to communicate them to the professors who will be writing your recommendations.

NEVER CHEAT ON THE ONES YOU LOVE

All schools have some departments that are less popular than others. So everyone thinks that saying you want to major in an undersubscribed department can help you get admitted. But not as a transfer. Because you have already been in college for a year or two or even three, schools expect you to have begun serious work in one area of interest. They will distrust any attempts to switch majors midstream. Not only will they doubt your motives, but schools want to accept students who will graduate in four years. Given the problems of arranging transfer credit, switching majors can be a nightmare.

Schools have also begun instituting rules that make it even more difficult to cheat on your application. The following is an excerpt from a U.C. Berkeley pamphlet for transfer students:

If I put down an uncrowded major just to get into Berkeley, can I switch after I'm in?

Your chances of making such a shift are extremely limited. [The College of] Letters and Science, for example, requires a student to remain in the original major for one year before being eligible to change to another major. The best advice is to plan for your transfer early and carefully, put down your true first choice major when you apply, and see what happens. . . . Trying to outwit the system is risky, and the stakes are high.

You can still use the system to your advantage, however, by avoiding schools where the department in which you are currently majoring is *oversubscribed.*

If you are transferring because you want to switch majors, it is critical that you explain in your application that your present school does not offer the major you are seeking or has a very weak department. Not all schools are as stringent about changing majors as Berkeley. Anne Woodruff transferred to Smith from Colorado College as an English major. And although all of her credits transferred, she found out later that none of them would count toward her English degree. She would have had to repeat the same classes she had taken at Colorado to fulfill Smith's departmental requirements. Instead, she changed her major from English to American Studies and encountered far fewer problems. Call your department to find out about credit policies and the rights of transfer students to switch majors after enrolling.

IVY ETIQUETTE

There is an unwritten rule among the Ivies not to accept transfers from other schools in the League. The general feeling is that transferring is supposed to give students who would not otherwise have the chance an opportunity to attend one of the nation's most prestigious schools. It is assumed that if you are already at an Ivy, you cannot possibly have an academic reason for transferring. Yearning to be in the country while stuck in Philadelphia won't get you admitted to Dartmouth.

At least not usually. Some students do transfer from one Ivy League school to another, but they are certainly the exception. And they almost always transfer for departmental reasons. Since Brown is the only Ivy to offer Egyptology (and the department is undersubscribed), a student who transfers to major in that field might very well get accepted.

INTERVIEWS

The interview serves two purposes: to let you learn more about the school and to let the school learn more about you. Although most schools do not require on-campus interviews for transfer applicants, it is definitely in your best interest to have one. As the Mount Holyoke transfer coordinator said, "The interview is a valuable opportunity to swap information and give the admissions officer a greater sense of the person behind the grades and numbers."

If your academic record is below average, a wonderful interview is not going to get you in. But if your credentials are borderline, it can only help. An interview is the easiest way to establish a solid rapport with an admissions officer and communicate directly your valid, compelling reasons for applying.

The interview allows you to explain exactly why you want to attend this particular institution, which professors you hope to study with, and what qualities you will bring to the community. It is a good time to demonstrate your research without showing off what you know. "Don't flaunt your preparation," says Anthony Medely in *Sweaty Palms,* a guide for trepid interviewees. "If you've done your research and preparation, it'll come across to the interviewer in the natural course of the interview. You will convey possession of knowledge and information through your demeanor and reactions to questions."[1]

Undoubtedly the interviewer will ask you questions like "So, why do you want to come to Purdue?" Your first reaction may be "Because I hate where I am now." But complaining about your current school is counterproductive. You want to be remembered as a positive, pleasant individual, not a whiner. Instead of griping, take the opportunity to cite several specific reasons why you want to spend two years in Indiana.

The key to a successful interview is research. Harvard's transfer coordinator told us about one student who wanted to transfer to Harvard in order to study Existentialism. He was a strong candidate with a valid academic reason for transferring, and yet he was denied admission. Why? Harvard does not offer any courses in Existential philosophy. How well you know the school will be immediately apparent to your interviewer. To make a good impression, you must be informed. In order to be well prepared, schedule the interview later in the year rather than earlier.

In addition to helping the school learn about you, the interview provides an opportunity for you to learn about the school, especially the details of transfer credit. Nevertheless, don't waste time asking questions that can be answered with a simple phone call. Find out about general transfer admissions policies before you arrive for the meeting.

Finally, always send a thank-you note to your interviewer.

1. Anthony Medely, *Sweaty Palms: The Neglected Art of Being Interviewed* (Berkeley, CA: Ten Speed Press, 1984).

RECOMMENDATIONS

Colleges ask for professor recommendations in order to gain insight into your academic ability. They are looking for additional information about your performance in college. Don't send old high school teachers' recommendations. Admissions committees want to see a recent evaluation of your accomplishments and will ignore anything else. The best recommendations are always from professors in your department, so don't ask an English professor to evaluate your work if you are majoring in Chemistry.

If you don't feel any professors know you or your work, try asking teaching assistants. In large schools with huge introductory classes, TAs are the ones who read papers, lead sections, and evaluate final grades. Schools want details, so only ask for recommendations from people who know you well. A general, impersonal account by a professor in a class where you got an A is not as good as an in-depth review of your strengths and weaknesses by a TA in whose class you got a B. Nevertheless, recommendations from professors are preferable, so get to know one or two.

Both professors and TAs will be able to write much stronger recommendations if they know why you are transferring. Try to spend at least fifteen minutes with each person to discuss your reasons for applying, your major, your career plans, and your academic history. Don't be shy; admissions officers need to learn as much about you as they can.

TRANSCRIPTS

Along with your application, you must provide the admissions office with a copy of your college transcript. Obtaining a transcript from the registrar's office can take from one or two days to several weeks, so order it early. If you have taken any classes Pass/Fail, be sure that your transcript indicates what constitutes a passing grade.

In most cases, you will also need to send an official copy of your high school record. This must be sent directly from your secondary school guidance counselor. Don't send high school recommendations or other material that was included in your original application.

STANDARDIZED TESTS

SAT and ACT scores are not as important in the transfer process as they are in standard admissions. The purpose of those exams is to predict how well students will perform academically in college. Since a transfer student *has* a college record, it will be weighted more heavily than high school SATs. Generally speaking, the longer you have been out of high school, the less your standardized test scores count. **A high GPA in college always overrides low test scores.**

Nevertheless, they are still required. If you graduated high school within the last several years, you do not need to take the tests again and may submit your original scores. Of course, you may retake the tests as many times as you like. High scores may not compensate for a poor college transcript, but they never hurt. Call the College Board for testing times and locations.

ATHLETES
National Collegiate Athletic Association Regulations

The number of NCAA regulations regarding eligibility for transfer athletes is mind-boggling, so we have tried to sift through the material in order to present the basic rules. Generally speaking, a student who transfers to a NCAA member institution must wait one academic year before being allowed to play on a varsity team. This "residence requirement" was instituted to discourage coaches from recruiting student athletes from other colleges. If you are transferring from a lower division school to a higher one (i.e., Div. II to Div. I), you can get around this residency requirement by obtaining permission from a coach at your original school. Otherwise, a student is exempted from the residency requirement if he or she

(1) transfers from a Division III school;

(2) is a foreign exchange student sponsored by the U.S. State Department, Rotary International, the Ford Foundation, the Institute of International Education, or a similar organization;

(3) transfers "in order to continue a major course of study because the original institution discontinued the academic program in the student's major";

(4) is returning from at least eighteen months of active service in the armed forces (while not concurrently enrolled in school) or from at least eighteen months of active service in an official church mission;

(5) transfers from a school that no longer offers the student's sport in its intercollegiate program;

(6) transfers from a school that has reclassified the sport from Division I to Division III and has not competed in the sport at the Division III level;

(7) has not played on a team for two years prior to the date on which the student begins participation;

(8) is returning to his or her original school after having transferred once to a school where he or she did not participate in a sport;

(9) was not recruited, received no athletically related financial assistance, and never participated in intercollegiate athletics (other than preseason try-outs) prior to transferring;

(10) plays a sport other than basketball, football, or men's hockey; has never transferred before; did not receive athletically related financial assistance from his or her first school (or that assistance has been discontinued, or the student was dropped from the team); is in good academic standing; transfers from a school that certifies in writing that it has no objection to the student's being granted a waiver to the residency requirement.[2]

2. NCAA Eligibility Rules. Transfer Regulations, section 14.6 (1989).

Permission from a coach must be in writing and sent to the Director of Athletics at your new school. In addition to this host of regulations, there are separate rules regarding students who transfer to and from two-year colleges; those rules are included in Chapter 7.

For more information regarding NCAA rules, try contacting a coach or the Director of Athletics at your new school. He or she may not be willing to talk to you, however, for fear of being accused of illegal recruiting. If your own coach can't help you, call the NCAA's legislative services at (913) 384-3220.

ROLLING ADMISSIONS

Some schools offer a policy of **Rolling Admissions** for transfer students. Admission is on a first-come, first-serve basis; you can apply as early or as late as you want, sometimes even during course registration at the beginning of the semester. If the school you want to go to doesn't have a specific admissions deadline, rejoice. Use the extra time to make your application as strong as possible. Remember, of course, that the earlier you apply, the better your chances of admission, getting housing, and arranging transfer credit.

UNTIL WE MEET AGAIN

Even if you're absolutely positive that any other college will be better than your present school, it is very important to leave open the option of returning. You don't have to tell your school you are transferring in order to leave. You can tell them you are spending a guest year at another institution or taking time off to work. Filing for a temporary leave of absence allows you to keep all of your options open.

There is no need to worry that your current school will somehow discover that you are really transferring. Registrars don't have the time or inclination to investigate your educational plans. Even when you ask the registrar's office for a copy of your official transcript, they won't conclude that you are transferring. You may be applying for a job, internship, or foreign study program.

If, however, you do inform your school that you are actually transferring, you may run into considerable difficulty later. Students who formally withdraw from an institution and wish to return are required to reapply as a transfer. Not only would this cost you time and money, but there is a chance that you might not get back in.

EXPERIMENTATION— VISITING STUDENT PROGRAMS

Some people try to visit another school for a semester or a year, hoping this will aid them in transferring. In reality, it does just the opposite. Schools actively discourage visiting students from applying to transfer. The intent of **visiting programs** is to give students an opportunity to sample another school's curriculum, not to help them matriculate. The admissions criteria for visiting students are usually much less stringent than for transfers, so even if you've done well academically during your guest year you won't be guaranteed admission. In fact, schools often have policies that require you to return to your original school for a year before you are even eligible to reapply as a transfer. Visiting can cost you a lot more time than it's worth.

TRANSFER CREDIT

By far the most trying element of switching schools is arranging **transfer credit.** Yet very few students anticipate the problems they will encounter. Almost no one thinks about transfer credit during their research or reapplication. Even fewer actively plan ahead. Each school has its own policies, but there are several steps you can take to earn all the credit you deserve.

Transfer credit is generally awarded on a course by course

basis. Blanket credit is rarely given, even for an associate's degree. There are exceptions, of course, but most of the time you will have to negotiate credit for each course you have taken.[3] Schools try to match your courses with comparable courses in their curriculum. The more you know about their academic system and distribution requirements, the better.

Don't be intimidated by university bureaucracy. Find out about your target school's transfer policies early so you can be prepared to fight for the credits you deserve. It's worth it. Making up credit requirements can cost you a summer, a semester, or even a year.

Validation Material

When you apply to transfer, the admissions office presents the school registrar with your transcript. The registrar makes a preliminary evaluation of your transcript and then consults various faculty members in order to determine exactly which classes are transferable. Together, they are trying to determine which of your courses are similar or *equivalent* to classes offered by their school. You can help by providing them with evidence demonstrating the equivalency of each of your courses.

The first step to winning transfer credit is compiling a **Suggested Course Equivalency Chart** (for an example, see p. 86). This chart lists your classes and the classes offered by your target school that are similar to them. To make this chart, you will need a copy of your transcript and the new school's course catalogue. For each of your classes, list a class offered by your target school that covers approximately the same material. If you cannot find a course that is similar to one you have taken, choose a class that covers different material but is of equal difficulty, or write "Independent Study." Also include information about any advanced placement exams you may have taken during high school. Rules regarding AP credit vary greatly from school to school. So even if you didn't qualify before, you may now be able to earn credit for your AP scores.

On a separate page, describe your **Projected Academic Program** (see p. 87). This is a list of all courses you plan to take at the second school and what requirements they will fulfill. The Projected Academic Program allows the registrar

3. The University of Oregon, for example, grants blanket credit for any Oregon junior college graduate with the AA degree. The university also assumes that the student has met the school's general education requirements for graduation.

and faculty to see how your previous courses will fit into your future plans. Plus, it demonstrates your familiarity with their educational system.

The third step to receiving credit is providing your target school with **course syllabi,** for all classes that may be in dispute. A syllabus is a detailed course description that usually indicates the required reading and the material to be covered each week of the semester. Save everything that demonstrates the level and content of a course; you may still be fighting for credit three months after you transfer. But don't panic if you have lost all your syllabi and cannot get them from professors or friends. For each class send a brief course description and a reading list. Keep copies of all validation material in case the registrar loses anything.

Send the Suggested Course Equivalency Chart and the Projected Academic Program along with all syllabi to the admissions office, or give the packet to an admissions officer directly in an interview (do not give it to an alumni interviewer). Staple syllabi together neatly with your name on each sheet and include a cover letter explaining the packet. Finally, include a copy of your present school's course catalogue with classes you have taken clearly marked. This is your **Transfer Credit Packet** and you should keep a copy of its entire contents.

As a last resort, if the registrar won't accept a course for which you think you deserve credit, ask the professor of the course to send a **letter on your behalf.** The professor may say no, but you have nothing to lose by asking. And don't worry about sending material that is not specifically asked for. Schools appreciate foresight and will use everything you give them.

Evaluation

The number of credits that is accepted by the registrar is called your total **transferable credit.** Many schools do not calculate final transfer credit until you have actually enrolled, but you have the right to a written evaluation, at least one month prior to enrolling, of your transferable credits (see the **Statement of Transfer Students' Responsibilities and Rights** on p. 92). This preliminary evaluation should give you some sense of your academic standing before you arrive on campus.

Most colleges and universities have a limit to how many transfer credits you can use toward a baccalaureate degree. They also have explicit residency requirements.

If you are applying to a large university that is composed of separate colleges, chances are there won't be a general policy regarding transfer credit. You will have to make arrangements with the particular college to which you are applying. Since each college has its own rules and regulations, it is important to get in touch with the registrar directly for an evaluation.

In the Interview

The interview is a good opportunity to discuss transfer credit, so bring along a copy of your Transfer Credit Packet. Since some schools leave all credit arrangements to the discretion of the registrar, it is a good idea to call ahead to see if your interviewer will be able to give a preliminary evaluation of your courses.

You should examine the school's course catalogue, in order to estimate the equivalency of your courses, before the interview. The meeting will be far more productive if you are informed. But if it looks like transfer credit is going to be a problem, don't argue. This is not the time to fight for each course. You certainly don't want the interviewer to write "antagonistic and hostile" on your folder. Rather, take note of which classes are questionable, so you will be better prepared to support your case later.

Final Calculation

Once you have been notified of your transferable credits, you still must convert those credits from your first school's system to the system of your new college. Schools use a whole range of credit systems. Although most colleges assign three or four credits per class, some schools use a quarter system and others use a block system where each course counts for one credit. The **conversion equation** below allows you to convert credits from an hour, semester, or quarter plan to any other arrangement.

Divide your transferable credits by the total number of credits required for graduation at your first school, and then multiply this number by the total number of credits required for graduation at your new school. The product is the number of credits you will enter with at your new school, your **new credit standing**.

Conversion Equation

$$\frac{\text{Transferable credits}}{\begin{array}{c}\text{Total no. of credits}\\\text{required for graduation}\\\text{at first college}\end{array}} \times \begin{array}{c}\text{Total no. of}\\\text{credits required}\\\text{for graduation}\\\text{at new college}\end{array} = \begin{array}{c}\text{New}\\\text{credit}\\\text{standing}\end{array}$$

For example, you have 60 transferable credits (out of 120 needed to graduate at your first school) and to graduate from your new school you need 30 units. Then you divide 60 by 120, which equals ½, and multiply ½ by 30 to get 15. When you arrive at your new school, you will have completed 15 units toward graduation.

After It's Over

Students are often surprised to learn after an ordeal of fighting for transfer credit that courses taken at one school don't even show up on the final transcript of another. When you graduate, your transcript will only list those courses taken at that school. Sometimes it will show courses that you never actually took but were equivalent to ones you took at your first school. Moreover, your final GPA will not include grades you received before transferring.

SUGGESTED COURSE EQUIVALENCY CHART

Caroline Hansen
Boston College to Wellesley College

History Major		Equivalent Wellesley Course	
Sem. I			
HS 81	Modern European History	HS 201	Mod. European History
EN 21	Critical Reading & Writing	EN 101	Critical Interpretation
TH 9	Fundamentals of Judaism	RS 140	Introduction to Judaism
MU 176	Music of the Romantic Era	MU 210	The Romantic Era
Sem. II			
HS 82	Mod. European History	HS 201	Mod. European History
EN 21	Critical Reading & Writing	EN 101	Critical Interpretation
PS 44	Psychology of Art	PH 203	Philosophy of Art
TA 25	Introduction to Communications	Independent Study	
Sem. III			
HS 181	American Civilization	HS 309	Social History of the U.S., 1600–1850
TH 253	Theology of Peace	PH 330	Seminar: Nuclear Ethics
BI 110	General Biology/Lab	BS 109	Human Biology/Lab
PO 321	Amer. Constitutional Law	APL 210	Law & Admin. Justice
Sem. IV			
HS 182	American Civilization	HS 309	Soc. History, 1877–1985
FA 257	Modern Art: 19th Century	HA 219	19th Century Art
HS 214	Modern South Africa	HS 263	South Africa in Historical Perspective
TH 88	Person & Social Responsibility	PH 210	Social Philosophy

Total Courses = 16

Projected Academic Program
Caroline Hansen
Boston College to Wellesley College

History Major: Focus on Women

257 Women in American History
241 Women in European History
231 History of Rome
271 Modern Japan
336 Hidden Bonds of Womanhood
364 Seminar: Women in Islamic Society

Distribution Courses

336 Women, the Family & the State (Amer. Politics & Law)
103 Introduction to Astronomy (Astr.)
206 Basic Astronomical Techniques (Astr.)
125 Writing

Electives

250 Asian Women in America (Women's Studies)
212 Black Women Writers (Black Studies)
102 Survey of Modern Economics (Econ.)
201 Micro Economic Analysis (Econ.)
212 History of American Education (Ed.)
121 Introduction to Shakespeare (Eng.)

Foreign Language Requirement

French Achievement score: 650

Physical Education Activities

Canoeing
CPR
Water Polo
Diving

Total Courses = 20

About the Sample Charts

Caroline's Suggested Course Equivalency Chart is fairly straightforward. Because she took many introductory classes at Boston College, she had little problem finding equivalent courses at Wellesley. Many of her B.C. requirements were two-semester courses, so she had to find several year-long courses at Wellesley as well.

Note that she could not find any course at Wellesley entitled Psychology of Art. Looking through the catalogue, she chose Philosophy of Art instead. If the registrar disputes the class, she will send a course syllabus and could suggest that another Psychology class (such as Psychology of Language) be considered.

In all likelihood, Caroline won't receive credit for her Communications class since Wellesley does not offer any similar class and only gives credit for liberal arts courses. Nevertheless, by writing "Independent Study" and by providing evidence of the depth and level of the course, she increases the chances that it will be seriously considered.

The registrar may dispute American Civilization as well, but the class was a requirement for History majors at B.C., so Caroline deserves the credit. The problem is that Social History is an upper-level class and American Civilization isn't. Unless American Civilization was an extremely rigorous class, Caroline probably shouldn't submit the syllabus until the registrar asks for it.

Finally, Theology of Peace and Seminar in Nuclear Ethics on page 86 sound like two very different classes, but in fact their descriptions in the course catalogues are practically identical. And although one is a 200-level class and the other a 300-level class, the numbering systems used by the two schools are different, so that a Boston College 200 level is equal to a Wellesley 300 level. Caroline may want to point this out in her cover letter.

The Projected Academic Program not only demonstrates Caroline's familiarity with the school but also illustrates clearly why she wants to attend. Any admissions officer looking at the chart would see immediately that Caroline is interested in studying women's history, a strong point in the Wellesley curriculum. In addition, the chart provides evidence that Caroline can complete all the Wellesley graduation requirements in two more years. Finally, her electives show that she will pursue a well-balanced, yet focused, course of study. Caroline's Projected Academic Program will clearly strengthen her overall application.

SUMMER SCHOOL

Unfortunately, students sometimes do lose whole semesters' worth of credit when classes won't transfer. To graduate in four years, you may have to attend summer school classes. It is a good idea during your research to find out if your school gives credit for summer classes taken anywhere or only at particular institutions. Brown University, for instance, only accepts summer school courses taken at Brown or at a college on a trimester system. You may even want to take classes at your target school the summer before you reapply to increase your chances of admission.

INTERCAMPUS TRANSFERRING

Rather than transferring to a completely new school, some students opt to move from one campus to another within the same university. **Intercampus transferring** is common in the University of California and State University of New York systems. The greatest advantage of intercampus transferring is the ease of arranging transfer credit. Plus, staying within a university demands less time in readjustment. Applying can be just as complicated, however, so act early.

A similar option is moving from one undergraduate college to another on the same university campus. Lauren Murray transferred from the School of Arts and Sciences to Hotel Management without ever leaving Cornell. She realized during her first year of school that she wanted to pursue a career in management. Lauren had a much easier time transferring than would someone who was applying from another university. Cornell facilitates this arrangement by allowing students to enroll concurrently in two undergraduate schools before actually transferring.

Reapplication Check List

☐ Obtain a Transfer Application form

☐ Find out about minimum requirements, residency, and transfer credit

☐ Ask two professors for recommendations

☐ Schedule an alumni or on-campus interview, and send a thank-you note

☐ Order your SAT or ACT scores

☐ Order your college and high school transcripts

☐ Ask your coach for permission to play after transferring

☐ File for a temporary "leave of absence"

Transfer Credit

☐ Send your **Transfer Credit Packet** validation materials:
 • Suggested Course Equivalency Chart
 • Projected Academic Program
 • Syllabi
 • Course Catalogue
 • Cover Letter

☐ Contact an admissions officer for a preliminary evaluation

☐ Send a final thank-you note to the admissions office

PETER GRAF
Tufts University to Columbia University

One month after transferring to Columbia, Peter Graf still didn't have housing. He was constantly moving, sleeping on friends' floors and in lounges. "It was absolutely hellish. My first semester would have been so different if I had been on campus." Transfer students are on the bottom of Columbia's housing list and are left to deal with finding apartments in New York City alone.

Peter abandoned the security of four years of guaranteed housing at Tufts because he wanted a more intellectual, diverse, and urban environment. He found the students too homogeneous and superficial. "People there were very pre-professional, and no one ever talked about what they were learning." He tried switching majors from Engineering to Philosophy, but he still felt out of place. Eventually, he decided that it was time to move back home to New York. "There was nothing to do in Somerville, and getting to Boston wasn't as easy as the brochures had promised."

Peter started the reapplication process early and didn't tell anyone of his decision. "In some ways it was totally impulsive." He didn't know that much about Columbia, other than that the school was "more diverse than Tufts and offered a challenging curriculum." Nevertheless, he was confident of his decision and chose not to apply to any other schools. "The one thing I was sure of was that I needed to be in New York."

Yet once he was accepted, Peter was hesitant to leave Tufts. "I started to think, 'I might find a niche here.' Actually, I was excited about my courses for sophomore year and my housing was settled." Transferring meant leaving everything familiar behind. After a great deal of agonizing, Peter decided to trust his gut feelings.

All in all, Peter had a rough first semester at Columbia. He wasn't immediately excited about his classes and it took time to get used to Columbia's demanding core curriculum. But once the housing crisis was settled, he began to appreciate the school. He found the intellectual climate at Columbia more rigorous and the students more self-motivated. Discussing ideas became an intrinsic part of his life. "Not like we talked about Plato and Freud every night, but the general attitude was more intellectual."

Still, Peter had to adjust to Columbia's "scattered social scene." He found that life did not center around the university and sometimes it was difficult to feel part of a community. Yet ultimately he thinks the advantages and intensity of Manhattan more than compensated. "I love the anonymity of New York—I can just get lost in a crowd and feel happy." And although transferring proved challenging, Peter says he would definitely do it again. "Columbia has made a profound, positive impact on how I view the world and my place in it."

TRANSFER STUDENTS' RESPONSIBILITIES AND RIGHTS

Hopefully, transferring will be a smooth, easy process. But just in case anything goes wrong, it's a good idea to know your rights. The National Association of College Admissions Counselors (NACAC) adopted the following statement to help all transfer students understand their responsibilities and rights in regard to transfer admissions.

Statement of Transfer Students' Responsibilities and Rights in the College Admissions Process

YOU HAVE THE RESPONSIBILITY:

To be aware of the policies (deadlines, restrictions, etc.) regarding admissions, transfer of courses and financial aid of colleges and universities of your choice.

To complete and submit required material to college and universities.

To meet all application deadlines.

To notify the colleges and universities which have offered you admission, of your acceptance or rejection of their offer as soon as you have heard from all to which you have applied, or by May 1, whichever is earlier.

YOU HAVE THE RIGHT:

Prior to applying, YOU HAVE THE RIGHT *to complete information from member NACAC colleges and universities concerning all policies and procedures involving:*

Transfer student's admissions requirements and documents required for admission and financial aid assistance.

Application fees, deposits, refunds and housing.

Transfer of courses, credit hours and quality points.

Transferability of courses with grade below a "C," and how these grades will affect the student's cumulative grade point average.

Transferability of courses repeated and credit previously granted by examination and advanced placement.

After official notification of acceptance, YOU HAVE THE RIGHT *to a written evaluation, at least one month prior to enrolling, of:*

Courses accepted for transfer credit and their course equivalency.

Which transfer courses will meet basic requirements for the degree you are seeking.

Your cumulative grade point average, number of quality points, if transferable, number of (semester/ quarter) hours transferred, and how many semesters/ quarters will be needed to complete degree requirements in currently stated major areas of study.

YOU HAVE THE RIGHT *to defer responding to an offer of admission and/or financial aid until you have heard from all colleges and universities to which you have applied, or until May 1, (whichever is earlier).*

Should you be denied this right: (1) immediately request the college/university to extend the reply date; (2) notify your counselor and ask him/her to notify the President of the State or Regional ACAC. For additional assistance, send a copy of your admission notification letter and all correspondence to:

Executive Director
NACAC
9933 Lawler Avenue, Suite 500
Skokie, Illinois 60077

Chapter 5

The Love Letter

THE SIX-STEP PLAN TO SUCCESSFULLY CHANGING SCHOOLS

BREAKING UP
Reevaluation

TELLING THE FOLKS
Renegotiation

PLAYING THE FIELD
Research

MAKING THE FIRST MOVE
Reapplication

WRITING THE LOVE LETTER
Revision

STARTING OVER
Readjustment

> *Christian: I love you.*
> *Roxane (closing her eyes): Yes, speak to me*
>   *of love.*
> *Christian: I love you.*
> *Roxane: That's the theme—now elaborate on*
>   *it.*
> *Christian: I love . . .*
> *Roxane: Develop your theme.*
> *Christian: I love you . . . so much.*
> *Roxane: Go on!*
>   *—Edmond Rostand,* Cyrano de Bergerac

"Why do you want to come here?" is the most important question asked on all transfer applications. The essay is your opportunity to state clearly and in your own words why you have decided to transfer. More specifically, it is a prime occasion to communicate to the admissions office your valid and compelling reasons for applying to their school. (As we said earlier, reasons are valid if they are academic and compelling if they demonstrate why you have chosen this *particular* school.) The essay also reveals your writing ability, an extremely important factor in the admissions process. You cannot change your transcript, but you can control the way in which you present yourself. For this reason alone, the transfer essay is critical.

REVISION
Writing the Transfer Essay

You cannot re-use your original college essay. It may have gotten you in the first time around, but transfer admissions officers do not want to hear about your first trip abroad and how it changed your life. Your essay must express your revised feelings about college, how they have changed since you applied the first time.

"A transfer's essay should be more sophisticated than a freshman applicant's," says Eric Widmer, Dean of Admissions at Brown University. "It's an important opportunity to explain why you want to leave and why you want to come to *our* school."

The essay also allows you to discuss what you will contribute personally to the institution. Although your essay must never read like a résumé, it can serve as a gentle reminder of your own strengths and accomplishments. Still, the content of the essay should explain and justify your decision to transfer, not just reveal one aspect of your personality. While some schools may offer open-ended essay topics, you should always use the personal statement to answer why you are transferring.

INTIMACY

A good transfer essay should read like a good love letter. It must be exquisitely personal. "I love you so much, please let me in" does not qualify as an effective billet-doux. Admissions committees will only be wooed by valid and compelling reasons for transferring.

The essay should be the culmination of your research. It is a chance to show your intimate knowledge of the school and its unique characteristics. To do so, you should synthesize and refine all of the information you gathered from reading primary and secondary sources, visiting the campus, and talking to students and faculty. Nevertheless, the same is true for the essay as for the interview: *avoid flaunting your knowledge*. Since excessive empty flattery is always immediately apparent, you will only want to mention those aspects of the school that you find truly alluring. The key is to be honest, subtle, and specific.

PASSION AND PERSPECTIVE

As a transfer applicant, you are undoubtedly passionate about your desire to change schools. Certainly, you have strong feelings about your first college. More important, you are committed to your new one and you want to communicate that commitment to the admissions office. Whoever is reading your essay expects to find a certain degree of critical perspective in the writing that is the mark of a mature, thoughtful individual.

Therefore, your transfer essay requires a skillful blend of passion and perspective.

You will prove the extent of your passion by the depth of your research. Explaining that you wish to study under a particular professor will reveal your excitement about the college. Discussing what you thought of a certain editorial piece in the campus newspaper will illustrate your enthusiasm. If you have thoroughly researched your target school, you will have no trouble displaying your passion.

Perspective is often more difficult to express. The gap between the senior year of high school and the first year in college is enormous, and admissions committees want to see a development in your attitude. You must show how one or two or three years of college have shaped your values. Yet you don't want to write about how college has dramatically altered the way you perceive global peace and social change. Keep your subject small. Trish Bilder brilliantly demonstrated perspective by using two diary entries as her essay. The differences between the one written from senior year of high school and the other from her second semester at Northwestern clearly illustrated her growth over a year. However you choose to do it, focus on how your educational goals and attitudes have changed.

As a transfer student, you have an objectivity about collegiate life that high school students often lack. It is important to show that objectivity in your writing. You realize that college isn't perfect and that one institution cannot possibly fulfill all your needs. But after being dissatisfied somewhere else you have chosen this particular college for very specific reasons. You know exactly what you are looking for and why. Use that distance to build a convincing argument for why you and this school are just right for each other.

BEYOND SEDUCTION

Courtly love requires more than just dainty kisses. To win your reader's heart, you should be persistent and aggressive. The essay must not only express your love, it must bid for your reader's love in return. Therefore you have to argue your case. There are two writing methods traditionally labeled the style of argument: **deductive** and **inductive.** Every love letter falls into one of the two categories and sometimes both.

Whichever style you choose, you must first establish your thesis. A thesis is a one-sentence statement of your argument, usually your reasons for applying. Before you begin writing your essay, make a list of each of your reasons and then extract from the list a general theme, so that you can write in one sentence why you want to transfer.

Your thesis should also argue why you ought to be admitted. In other words, it should fall somewhere between "I want to transfer to your school because . . ." and "You should accept me for the following reasons . . ." The best thesis is both strong and subtle.

Some Sample Theses:

• Since graduating high school, I have discovered post-Freudian psychology, which I would like to study at Boston University because of the department's strong emphasis on feminist theory and the opportunity to work under Professor Jean Baker Miller.

• My work last summer with dyslexic children has inspired me to pursue linguistics and cognitive science, two areas that are particularly strong at Iowa State University where I hope to study next year.

• After one year at a southern school I have grown more aware of the diversity of American culture; now, I need the supportive environment of Oberlin where I will feel comfortable as a black woman to continue my preparation for a career in sociology.

Your thesis is only as strong as your evidence supporting it, so don't make claims that you cannot prove. The author of the last example, for instance, would want to demonstrate how Oberlin offers a "supportive environment," and why she has chosen that school to study sociology. Keep your thesis to the point; it is best to avoid both flattery and arrogance.

Deduction

The deductive essay states clearly, "I love you and this is why." Of the two argumentative styles, it is the easier. You state your general premise (thesis) early and then prove it point by point. Because of its direct, straightforward approach, the deductive method can be maintained for several pages or an entire book. Of course, the transfer essay should be no more

DEDUCTION

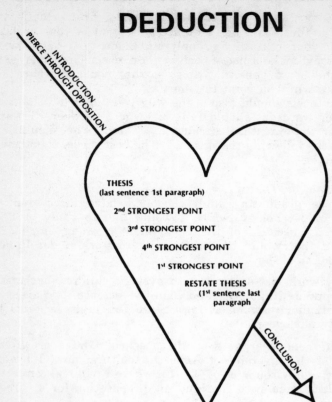

INTRODUCTION
PIERCE THROUGH OPPOSITION

THESIS
(last sentence 1st paragraph)

2nd STRONGEST POINT

3rd STRONGEST POINT

4th STRONGEST POINT

1st STRONGEST POINT

RESTATE THESIS
(1st sentence last
paragraph

CONCLUSION

than one page, beginning with a simple introduction and ending with a solid conclusion.

A deductive introduction leads up to and ends with the thesis, preferably the last sentence of your first paragraph. Each succeeding paragraph defends the thesis, proving through example, until the reader is convinced of the argument. Before the essay is over, the thesis strikes once again (at the beginning of the last paragraph) and then steps back, allowing the curtain to fall and the reader to smile.

Each paragraph of your essay should feature one or two examples drawn from your research that support your thesis. Arrange them in order so that your strongest point is last, your second strongest point is first, your third strongest point is second, your fourth strongest point is third, and so on. In other words, your weakest argument should be buried, directly before your strongest.

The trickiest element of deductive writing is overcoming a reader's objections to the thesis. The strongest essay considers and dismisses all objections in the first paragraph. For example, your premise is that you should be accepted because you are a wonderful actor and need to study theater in Chicago. However, your transcript shows that you never studied theater at your first school, so a reader probably will doubt the honesty of your argument. So in your introduction you should begin with an explanation of why you chose not to perform during your first year of college. Perhaps the department was closed to nonmajors, or you were discriminated against for some reason. By confronting your reader's objections in the first paragraph, you clear the way to argue your case.

You may want to write your introduction last so that you can see as you write what objections a reader might raise. Many writers also find it easier to begin in the middle with the thrust of their argument rather than with the opening line. Don't spend too much time worrying about the conclusion, either; it should be just one or two last thoughts that will leave your reader feeling fulfilled.

As you write, remember to state your thesis at the end of your first paragraph and at the beginning of your last. Make sure that each of your points supports your thesis clearly. Finally, use topic sentences for each of your paragraphs to keep the essay coherent.

Induction

If the deductive essay begins by shouting, "I love you!", the inductive one takes a more subtle, romantic approach. It offers chocolates, then maybe flowers, perhaps an invitation to a dance, and finally a kiss. The inductive style works best in the hands of spy novelists, who can weave a suspenseful story, drop tantalizing clues along the way, and finish with a dramatic climax. Whereas the deductive essay reveals its thesis in the opening scene, the inductive one holds it secret like a prize until the very end.

Induction works well if you use a story to make your point. For example, Maggie Alexander's essay (see p. 107) begins with a short narrative about a classroom experience to explain why she wants to transfer from an all-female to a co-educational environment. Her story ends with her thesis.

In an inductive essay, examples are harder to illustrate than in a deductive one. You must supply evidence as part of the progression toward your thesis. (Or you can add your proof at the end, after you arrive at your main point. This creates the

INDUCTION

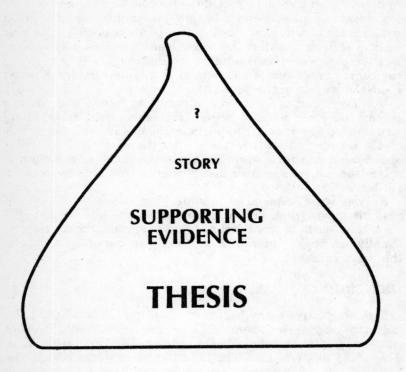

?

STORY

SUPPORTING EVIDENCE

THESIS

same effect as the final scene in a mystery movie when the detective reveals step by step how the thief committed the crime. Again, see Maggie's essay on p. 107.) You must pay special attention to your argument so that you don't let it slip by unproven.

You may want to begin with a question, such as "Why do I want to leave the familiarity of my home state to come to the challenging environment of Alaska?" If you try such an approach, be careful that you answer fully the question you have posed.

Induction is a harder style to master than its opposite, but it is usually more interesting to read. You may want to try a combination of the two, beginning with a short narrative that leads up to your thesis and concluding with a straightforward defense of your argument. Experiment until you find the style that is most effective for you.

Faux Pas

Spelling mistakes
Grammatical errors
Sloppiness
Sarcasm
Cursing
Name dropping
Whining
Complaining
Redundancy
Wordiness
Slang
Vulgarity
Jargon
Pretentiousness
Cynicism
Clichés

TRASHING YOUR EX

When writing the transfer essay, your first instinct might be to rant and rave about your current school's flaws. After all, it is the school's fault that the relationship failed, and you deserve pity for the trials you have endured. But no matter how strong your desire, don't blame the school.

Begin by taking responsibility for what went wrong. You may hate everything about your first school, but in the essay you must demonstrate how you have made the most of your time there. Stanford explicitly states in its brochures that it considers how well "an individual has taken advantage of available resources, whether an applicant has faced and withstood unusual adversity, and whether an applicant shows promise as a considerate, congenial roommate and a contributing dorm and community member." Colleges want evidence that you have been an active participant, not a passive victim. So, provide concrete examples of how you have tried to improve your situation.

Under no circumstances can your essay be a list of complaints, a plea for escape, or in the words of Admissions Counselor Kevin Barr, "a letter from prison." A good essay clearly articulates specific grievances while sustaining a spirited, positive tone. If you must criticize, do so constructively. Discuss which specific aspects of your current school you find unsatisfactory and why. "I felt the Communications Department was too theoretical" is much better than "The college was anti-intellectual." Remember many people are happy at that school. You have to explain why it isn't right for you.

The essay also presents a good opportunity to explain any poor grades on your transcript. The best reasons are ones that illustrate clearly why you were unable to succeed. "I was so depressed all the time I just couldn't study" won't win sympathy from an admissions officer. On the other hand, if you had a serious family crisis in the middle of the semester, you should cite that fact. And if you were bored by the simplicity of a French class that focused only on basic grammar and never discussed literature, you may want to mention that as well. Explain whatever the cause of your demise briefly and without exaggeration. Don't let your essay turn into a full-page apologia.

Whatever you say about your current school, only include critical details that are relevant to your reasons for applying. You can definitely mention your school's weak Chemistry Department as a reason for leaving, but your emphasis should be on your target school's fantastic science center and lab facilities. Never lose sight of your audience.

WILL YOU BE MY VALENTINE?

Clearly, you want to use the love letter to compliment your reader. And at the same time, it offers the perfect opportunity to explain why you want to change relationships midstream.

Since it is difficult to accomplish both tasks equally well, it makes sense to choose one as the thrust of your essay. (Of course, you always want to convey your personal strengths and charm as well.) Below are discussions of how to emphasize either flattery or explanation and examples of two successful essays.

Complimenting the Reader: "The Courtly Essay"

"How much do I love thee? Let me count the ways." Every admissions officer wants to know that you truly love his or her school, and for good reasons. "The Courtly Essay" serenades its reader with praise. As long as you are never brazen in your flattery, this essay is sure to entice and beguile.

Before you sit down to compliment your hoped-for school, review your research. You must know what attributes the school wants to be appreciated for. Does it pride itself on being a diverse, vibrant university or a small, specialized college? Use specific, concrete examples. It is fine to mention little quirks about a school that drive you wild, such as its beautiful campus and Gothic architecture, but never give the impression of being superficially infatuated, or worse, lustful. Illustrate that you love the school for its intellectual faculties.

MELANIE PANKO
Wheelock College–Boston College

When I began my initial search for a college, as a high school senior, I felt that only one criterion need be met. This was that the institution I attended had to provide a program that would help me develop into the best teacher I could be. I chose Wheelock College for its excellent reputation for producing quality teachers.

Upon my arrival, I eagerly delved into my studies. However, several weeks later I found myself lacking a workload. I was not being challenged. I approached my English and Education professors with my dilemma. In each class we outlined a program of additional studies that would force me to work harder. As the first semester continued, I still questioned the amount and difficulty of the work I was doing. I began to examine why I was not happy at Wheelock.

It was after several weeks of deep thought that I realized my ideas had changed. While I still felt that quality teaching was very important, I saw that I could not do that without a broad, strong background. A teacher of young children should have the capability to inspire her students to learn and explore the world of knowledge, inside and out of the classroom. Wheelock offers an excellent education program but the liberal arts area is for me narrow and not very challenging. I knew that somewhere strong programs in both areas were combined.

I chose to investigate Boston College for its reputation in both areas. I began by contacting two professors there, Mary Katherine Cronin and Dr. Lillian Buckley. I explained my situation and was encouraged to sit in on classes. The ENG 101 class I sat in on, which in theory would be similar to my ENG 101 class at Wheelock, was a different world. The students were studying poetry and being asked to analyze it. Analysis was something that was considered to be far above freshmen at Wheelock. We were doing grammar exercises. I left the class exhilarated and highly motivated. This is how I wanted to be learning.

After careful research, discussions with students and faculty at Boston College, and a discussion with my advisor at Wheelock, I decided Boston College could offer me the best of both worlds. The School of Education has an excellent reputation and I can obtain a challenging and diverse liberal arts background that is also important. I believe that an institution so dedicated to educating can help me become an excellent educator.

Melanie's essay is a superb example of a "Courtly" love letter. It is a clear statement of why she wants to attend Boston College, supported by specific details about the school. The essay demonstrates the seriousness of her decision and the extent of her research. She spoke with faculty members, visited classes, and consulted advisors. There is no question that Boston College is the right school for Melanie. (See her profile in Chapter 3.)

And although Wheelock was the wrong college, Melanie never blames it. Instead, she shows how her own goals have changed since high school. While she still wants to be a teacher, Melanie has discovered the value of the liberal arts, and clearly states how Boston College's education program will better serve her needs. Her reasons for applying are both valid and compelling.

In addition to complimenting Boston College and explaining her reasons for transferring, Melanie's essay reveals her own strengths and intellectual curiosity. Her efforts to try to improve her situation at Wheelock demonstrate that she is an assertive, self-reliant individual. Melanie is clearly passionate about learning and teaching, and will thrive in Boston College's rigorous intellectual environment.

Her essay is the ideal love letter, passionate about where she wants to be while maintaining perspective about the past. It is strong, rich with detail, and to-the-point.

Why I Want to Change Schools Midstream: "The Explanatory Essay"

Even if you have excellent reasons for applying, schools may be curious about your reasons for leaving your first college. If you feel the admissions office may question your motives, this essay will help you strengthen your position.

You don't want to rely on this form, however, if your reasons for leaving are not sufficient. An admissions officer probably won't respect your desire for better weather, or even your negative feelings about a school's social climate. But it is a good approach if you want to explain that you have to transfer for personal reasons, such as your parents moving, or mention that you are caught in an environment of racism or sexism. Don't begin cataloguing criticisms of your current school, however. Always write in a positive tone.

In almost all circumstances, a school is more interested in your reasons for applying than your reasons for leaving, so try to end on a "Courtly" note: "This is why I must attend your school." The more your essay strives to compliment its reader, the more successful it is sure to be.

MAGGIE ALEXANDER
Wellesley College–Brown University

The very eager women taking Images of Blacks and Women in Cinema had just finished viewing Spike Lee's She's Gotta Have It. *The guest speaker sauntered to the front of the room, approaching the blackboard in silence. As the words slowly began to take form, they soared from his fingers into my mind. "Negative images of black women," I read. This can't be what he means, nothing can be further from the truth. As if to reconfirm his absurdity, the self-proclaimed authority spoke, "Nola Darling is a freak."*

"This man has no chance," I thought. Twelve hands went up with lightning speed. I waited to speak with monastic fervor, while he rambled on—stifling conversation repeatedly. "This movie sends out a message that all black women have

insatiable sexual appetites," he concluded. I had never heard anything so inane before, and especially not at Wellesley. Not only had he taken up the remainder of our seminar time with his psycho babble but he allowed very little commentary from the class. He addressed only what he wanted to, and proceeded to impugn our arguments with a single glance. In one word, he seized control.

Black Studies 222 had never been this exciting. This pompous man, a guest in our forum, infuriated me. His opinions were maddening, and worst of all he failed to support them time after time. "Don't you think Nola's power has anything to do with her physical appearance?" I asked. "Absolutely not," he barked. Questions and comments flew at him like bullets, but, protected by his armor of authority, he controlled the class as well as who spoke when. As I left the seminar, I tried to comprehend what had just happened. "What a stifling situation," I thought at first. I was forced to rethink my own values in the light of the guest speaker's rubbish. "But wasn't that great?" I thought again. He poked holes into theories that I held sacred, and forced me to reevaluate everything.

As I replay this revelatory experience, I scan my bookshelf. In between the wooden planks sit my most valuable possessions: Jane Eyre, Their Eyes Were Watching God, Wide Sargasso Sea, *and* The Ballad of the Sad Café, *to name a few. Reading these books at the tail end of my high school career in a class named Gendered Society changed my life. It opened a world I never knew existed: Women's Studies.*

I awaited my entrance to Wellesley with enthusiasm. What better place to study Women's Studies than the best women's college in the country? But my experience here has been quite ironic. Although Wellesley offers an excellent Women Studies major, it is also accompanied by a comfortable security. It is very easy to be a feminist when that's what you're surrounded by. The place that gives women such fantastic opportunity and facility to learn also denies them the supreme experience of challenge. This missing shade of reality reflects the plight of the women's college. It lacks the intellectual stimulation that a coeducational environment nurtures. Although four years at Wellesley would yield a fine education, I desire an environment that more approximates the world at large. To me, Brown's New Curriculum, Women's Studies major, and Division One tennis program represent the ultimate challenge. I believe that Brown University can make me redefine what I hold to be true over and over again.

Maggie's essay blends passion and perspective. She begins with a personal story that leads, inductively, to why she wants to transfer. The story is compelling, her reasons are well thought out, and although she is critical of all-female schools, she never once complains about Wellesley.

While Maggie doesn't mention Brown until the very end of her essay, she maintains a sense of audience throughout. There was some risk in choosing such a political topic, but she knew that liberal politics are actively promoted at Brown. In fact, Women's Studies is an especially respected and academically rigorous department.

The narrative explains her reasons for attending Wellesley and traces her development as a feminist from high school. Note that it is not necessary to have seen the film *She's Gotta Have It* to understand the story. The essay is clear, well written, and demonstrates a college-level vocabulary.

Maggie's passion for learning is evident throughout. She describes books as her "most valuable possessions." Worried about being intellectually stagnant, she seeks a more challenging environment. In other words, her reasons for applying are valid and compelling, and she spells them out clearly in the last paragraph. Maggie's piece is an excellent example of a well-balanced transfer essay.

POSTSCRIPTS

It is sometimes tempting to send two or three essays with your application. You may feel more comfortable with fiction than expository writing or want to send an example of your academic work. Admissions officers, however, are busy individuals and are unlikely to take the time to read unsolicited writing samples. If you have a brilliant, creative piece of writing that you simply must send, don't despair. You may submit it as your official essay, so long as you accompany it with an addendum, stating briefly your reasons for applying. Emma Plunket, for example, wrote about how she tried to sell her mother to a bus driver when she was five. At the bottom of the page she wrote a few paragraphs explaining why she wanted to leave the University of Rochester and her need for Wesleyan's challenging academic environment and liberal political climate. Her essay was a success.

It is not necessary to fit your essay and addendum into the space provided on the application form, but don't use more than one additional page. Remember to print your name and address on any separate pages that you send with your application, and staple those pages to the form itself. In the space below the question, print "Enclosure" or "See Attached Sheet."

If your school does not require an essay, you should send one anyway. You must state your reasons for applying somewhere on the application. Since Fairfield University does not ask for an essay, Molly Bloom sent the following letter instead, in which she explains how she has spent the last year away from school. Because Molly had previously been accepted to Fairfield, she did not need to make her letter a full-fledged transfer essay.

David M. Flynn, Dean of Admissions   May 26, 1988
Office of Admissions
Fairfield University
Fairfield, Connecticut 06430-7524

Dear Dean Flynn:

Last week I had an interview with Rafael Mora and was informed that action on my file for transfer application would not be taken until you received my grades from this spring semester. Ramapo College will not be able to send my official grades for three weeks, but these are the grades I received from my teachers: Introduction to Psychology, 3 credits, B+; Western Studies 1, 4 credits, A−.

As you know, I have asked you to reactivate my file for transfer application. Last year after I had completed my freshman year studying architecture at Penn State I applied to transfer to Fairfield and was accepted but unfortunately did not enroll. Instead, I returned to Penn State and began my second year in the architecture program, but I was not interested in pursuing architecture.

I left Penn State, began working and teaching a religion class at my church, and when the spring semester came I decided to keep working and take seven credits at Ramapo College. I also began taking jewelry design class, and I was chosen to be "on team" to prepare a religious weekend called S.E.A.R.C.H.

I have decided that I am ready to go back to school. I know I still like art and design and I am very interested in obtaining a well-rounded liberal-arts education. Although I needed this last year away from school to grow up a little and redefine my goals, I am indeed sorry that I did not accept Fairfield's offer of admission a year ago. Please note that if given a second chance to attend Fairfield, I certainly will. I appreciate your reconsideration.

Sincerely,

Molly Bloom

MÉNAGE À TROIS

If you find that your heart simply belongs to two schools, or you are afraid to make the commitment to just one, be forewarned. Do not use the same essay for both schools. Of course, the idea of using the same essay should not even cross your mind: your first is tailored so closely to the school. Love letters can never be generic. As we said earlier, applying to two schools requires twice as much time.

A FINAL NOTE ON CHARM

Practice. Don't wait until the last minute to write your transfer essay. Charm isn't easy and it takes time to write eloquent prose. As Kit Reed says in her book on writing: "Working writers know there are no tricks, no special documents that automatically entitle a writer to success, but there is another way. It is revision."[1]

Give yourself enough time to rewrite and revise. Brighten your paragraphs with examples, and vary your sentence structure. Most important, always have other people read and criticize your work. Schools won't mind if you cannot spell, but they will think twice if you are too lazy to find a proofreader. And if you ever get bogged down in a sentence, or start to drown in a sea of signification, take the advice of Gertrude Stein in *How to Write:* forget grammar and think about potatoes.

---

1. Kit Reed, *Revision* (Cincinnati, OH: Writer's Digest Books, 1989).

Chapter 6

All New Problems

THE SIX-STEP PLAN TO SUCCESSFULLY CHANGING SCHOOLS

BREAKING UP
Reevaluation

TELLING THE FOLKS
Renegotiation

PLAYING THE FIELD
Research

MAKING THE FIRST MOVE
Reapplication

WRITING THE LOVE LETTER
Revision

STARTING OVER
Readjustment

STARTING OVER

Readjusting to a new school is the most important and most difficult part of transferring. Even when old problems disappear, new ones inevitably arise. No matter how hard we try to believe it, there is no such thing as a perfect relationship. But if the school you have chosen is just right for you, then the difficult days of readjustment should pass quickly.

Like all other aspects of transferring, readjustment is easier if you act strategically. Students who experienced difficult adjustments often look back and blame their own attitude or lack of effort. And as Maria Colt said about transferring from Wheaton to St. Lawrence, "It's just so hard being a new person and a sophomore." Starting over requires a lot of work as well as a great deal of patience. The nine suggestions given below should help you to adjust as smoothly as possible.

Hopefully, your school has a solid orientation program specifically designed for transfers. If not, don't worry. The greatest advantage of a good orientation program is that it allows you to meet other students who are as lost as you are. A little extra enthusiasm on your part can make up for a bad program.

Finding housing, arranging transfer credit, and making new friends are just some of the problems you will have to confront. Readjustment is a critical period: adapting to a new environment is inevitably stressful. You may panic and think that you've made the wrong decision. Transferring a second time may suddenly seem appealing, but it is almost always a bad idea. Remember, *you can make it work if you give it time.*

MID-YEARS

In September, transfer students aren't the only ones adjusting. First-year students arrive on campus completely unfamiliar with college life. But mid-year transfer students may feel even more alone. Schools accept transfer applicants for the spring semester because attrition rates tend to be greater in the spring than in the fall. Since so many students go abroad or take time off in the second half of the year, more housing is available. So, every January, a second group of transfers arrives on campus.

Mid-year readjustment isn't easy. Orientation programs are less formal and shorter than the ones offered in the beginning of the year. And since the number of new people is usually much smaller in the spring, there isn't the sense of everybody being lost together. The openness of the first week of school, when people are always introducing themselves, is over. By January, even fall transfers appear firmly established.

It can also be difficult to get involved with extracurricular activities because you feel like you're "jumping in midstream." But even if it seems as though everyone else is settled, remember that each semester is very different. Students are constantly starting over—taking time off, switching activities, returning from abroad, or joining new organizations. College groups are perpetually in flux and always in need of new people. In a few weeks you may even find yourself running the show.

The best advice is, don't be intimidated. College is not as impenetrable as it sometimes seems. But you can't wait for others to make the first move. All of the suggestions below apply equally to mid-year students. As long as you make the extra effort to be outgoing, you'll be "fine."

January Baby
(music and lyrics by Timothy Murphy and Melissa Levis)

I'm a mid-year
Is anybody here?
It's just me and my teddy
And a wet tear
And no comforting ear.
I've been abandoned already.

I'm a mid-year
And I want to disappear
'Cause this school is cold and lonely
I've got no friends here.
And I do fear
I wouldn't have come if they had told me.

The catalogue looked cheery, groovy and great.
I thought that it would be worth the wait
And so I passed up Wesleyan, Cornell and Penn State
I've been duped and it's nine months too late.

I feel conspicuous and out of place
And everyone else seems so cool
They tell me not to walk at night without my mace.
Gee, I never thought I'd miss high school.

So I'll stay here.
And feign good cheer
Smile and the world smiles with you.
And make it appear
I'm not a mid-year
And do what other kids do.

I've got my old friends
Who I know love me
They remind me of the good times.
And with their phone calls
It's not so bad at all
And I think maybe I'll be fine.
I think maybe I'll be fine.

NINE SUGGESTIONS FOR EASING THE TRANSITION

1. Plan Ahead

Readjustment begins long before you arrive on campus. As you say goodbye to friends at your first school, you may already feel regret. The best way to begin your reorientation is to stop analyzing your decision to leave. Don't continue to question whether or not your first school is right for you. As soon as you have completed the process of reapplication, allow yourself to enjoy the positive aspects of both schools. It is best to leave a college feeling complete about the experience, knowing that you have gotten as much out of it as you can and that you are ready to move on.

The summer or break before you re-enroll is an important time to begin the process of readjustment. Call one or two students you met during your research visit and talk to them about which classes to take and which activities to get involved in. Reread any school brochures you have lying around and certainly read all the new ones coming in the mail.

Try to complete all transfer credit arrangements before arriving on campus. If that's not possible, use the time to prepare for possible battles ahead. Collect syllabi, course descriptions, and letters from professors at your first school. Even if you have already been notified of your credit standing and have lost a semester (or a year), you may still be able to fight for credits when you arrive on campus. Just in case, however, this may be a good time to consider summer school.

The most important aspect of planning ahead is housing. Too many transfer students don't receive on-campus housing and allow this to spoil their entire year. Don't give up hope if you are denied housing right away, because all schools have wait lists. If you do get placed on a wait list, call the housing office to find out your chances of getting a room. Keep in mind that on-campus housing for transfers may be worse than an off-campus apartment. The earlier you start looking for off-campus housing, or ask others to look for you, the better your odds of getting a decent apartment.

Arranging off-campus housing from home is often very difficult, but it can be done. When Michael Becker found out that he couldn't get on-campus housing, he called the Gettysburg admissions office for a list of other transfer students. Getting four of those students to share an apartment with him made adjustment much easier. "We were constantly having transfer parties. We all had great stories about our old schools. It was a lot of fun."

The more familiar you are with your school, the sooner you will feel at home once you arrive. By handling transfer credit and housing beforehand, you can spend your first few weeks at your new college taking advantage of everything it has to offer.

2. *Don't Be Shy*

Everyone knows the hardest part of transferring is making friends. But being a transfer can actually make meeting people easier. You will immediately find a close group of friends amongst other transfers. This small and supportive community is particularly important if you transferred to a large university.

You will also be surprised by how interested non-transfer students will be in your experience. According to Sandra Simmons, "Transferring is a great topic of conversation, especially in interviews. It gives you a chance to talk about your goals and shows you can make difficult decisions." So, use your experience to meet other people. Sandra met her current boyfriend when asking for directions.

Some transfers told us they wanted to meet "regular" students, so they intentionally avoided spending time with other transfers. If you feel comfortable enough with your own sociability that you can afford to limit your acquaintances to one group, that's fine. But don't immediately dismiss anyone— other transfers, first-year students, or mid-years. Like you, transfer students are dynamic, assertive individuals with interesting stories to tell about their experiences. And, of course, you share a common bond.

Even if you are outgoing amongst your peers, it is often difficult to remember to meet faculty as well. Part of becoming acquainted with a school is getting to know professors outside of class. As a transfer you should make an extra effort to go to professors' office hours, faculty-sponsored events, and departmental meetings. You need to become familiar with your school's academic and advising systems. The only way you'll learn about which classes to take and how to avoid red tape is by asking lots of questions. Teaching assistants are also helpful resources in finding out about the college's opportunities.

It is important to seek out as much advice, from as many people, as you can. Meet with deans, administrators, and even alumni. In so doing, you will create a resource network that you can turn to immediately if you should run into problems later.

3. *Get Involved*

First-year students are often timid about participating in campus activities, and understandably so. As a transfer, however, you should not face problems of seniority or feel overwhelmed by the adjustment to college workloads. Get involved in one or two activities, and you will find adjustment comes naturally.

Extracurricular activities offer an instant group of friends. Jeffrey Shultz felt isolated from the community after transferring to NYU. To remedy the situation, he ran for dormitory president. "I pummelled the dorm with me," Jeffrey says. He knocked on everyone's door, promised more parties if elected, and won by a landslide.

Another route to getting involved is the Greek system. Many students purposely choose new schools with a chapter of their fraternity or sorority on campus. By living in-house you can avoid the hassles of both lotteries and landlords. Fraternities and sororities also provide an instant social circle. And even if you don't live in residence, as a member you can attend their parties and meetings. Staying Greek is often a good way to ease the transition between two schools.

An important part of belonging to a community is knowing how that community functions. Activities provide a way to learn about a school. Whatever group you join, you will quickly learn about school leaders, important faculty and administrators, and events on campus.

Of course, the most important reason to join a group is for the feeling of belonging it provides. The biggest problem that all new students face is feeling alienated from the main school community. As a member of a group you can put away the identity of a transfer for one closer to your personality.

4. *Explore*

It is surprising how few students at a college fully know their way around before senior year. Reorientation begins with finding your bearings. Explore your new school thoroughly, not just where your classes are located but the entire campus, even places you would never think of spending time. Check out sports fields, laboratories, office buildings, and other dormitories. Always feeling lost on campus is an unnecessary annoyance. The sooner you learn your way around, the better.

Also take advantage of your school's new location. If you're in a city, explore by both day and night. Go with a friend and be tourists for a day. In the country, enjoy the availability of outdoor sports and activities. Find out about student prices for local movies, theater, and museums. A good general rule is "The more you do, the more there is to do."

5. *Know Your School*

Since you will be arriving one or two years later than the average student, you will have to make up for the time you have lost in getting to know your school. Although your research should have made you feel as familiar with your school as a stranger can be, day-to-day living requires more extensive knowledge.

A good way to keep up with what's going on with other students is by reading campus publications: school newspapers, art and literary magazines, academic and political journals. You should know what your peers are thinking and writing about. Plus, campus periodicals are always looking, and sometimes begging, for new contributors; you certainly have nothing to lose by submitting. Understanding and participating in the intellectual life of your school is a vital aspect of readjustment.

You may also want to learn about your school's past. What are the major events in its history that give it its present character? Who were the people whose names are now engraved on the library? Many schools have extensive archives and some even have tape-recorded oral histories of alumni. If you're at all interested in history, these documents add a fascinating perspective to a college. Look into the possibilities of doing research and incorporating your school's past into your academic work.

The advantages of such knowledge are enormous. You will be able to take better classes, avoid bureaucratic hassles, feel more connected, and take advantage of all your college has to offer. Don't wait until you are a senior to be "culturally literate" about your school.

6. Don't Depend on Orientation Programs

Don't expect orientation to make you feel instantly readjusted. Since they only last a few days, these programs tend to be superficial. (They were your first year, too, you just didn't notice.) And although they may be fun, they probably won't be very informative. What transfer students usually find the most frustrating is that too many things are happening at once. As Alaina Wicks said, "It would have been helpful if the programs were given after we had gotten settled. In the first week nothing sunk in."

Often schools cannot afford to provide an orientation program just for transfers, so they place transfers in programs designed for first-year students. If you are arriving mid-year, this is less likely to happen. You can be fairly sure that if you *are* placed in a first-year program, at least a few events specifically for transfers should be offered as well. There is one large advantage to having orientation with first-year students, which most people don't realize: you get to meet three times as many people, all of whom will still be around your senior year.

By far the most useful aspect of orientation is the written information it provides—maps, advisors' phone numbers, calendars of social events, and notices about academic regulations and transfer credit. Save *all* the pamphlets you receive. After the excitement of the first week dies down, you are going to need to know practical things like who to talk to about designing an independent major.

If you have them, be sure to take advantage of transfer peer counselors. Student advisors should be able to answer all of the things you really want to know. What's the best pizza? Who are the most dynamic professors? Which bars are popular? How late can you drop a class? And where can you find an all-night diner?

7. Take Advantage of the School

You don't have to know where everything is on campus but you do have to know who to ask to find out. As a transfer you may have to put up with a lot of red tape. But university bureaucracies become a lot less intimidating if you're informed about what you want and persevere in getting it.

Sasha Silverman felt that the biggest problem she and her friends had was that "we weren't pushy enough to get what we wanted. When we got the run-around, we gave up." One woman wanted to join an honors program but was strongly discouraged against it. She found out too late that she was eligible and could have handled the schedule. Sasha experienced similar resistance when she tried to double-major. But even though her counselor insisted it wouldn't work, she was persistent and successful. So, don't give up when the first person you talk to says no. You transferred to get the most out of college. Be aggressive, and you will.

8. Go Back to Visit

When things are going particularly badly, you may panic and wonder, "Did I make a huge mistake?" Your old school suddenly looks wonderful in retrospect and transferring back seems like a great idea. If you find yourself getting nostalgic, go back and visit. You will be surprised how quickly you remember why you left. Visiting adds perspective and should stop you from romanticizing the past. The best cure for homesickness is to go home.

But what if after visiting you still want to go back? Terry Gilligan was unhappy at Northwestern because it was "too large and almost too diverse." She transferred to Colgate in upstate New York, which turned out to be "the opposite extreme." Terry immediately missed city life and decided to return after only one semester. Transferring back is easy as long as you have not officially transferred from your first school. Because Terry told Northwestern that she was taking a semester as a visiting student at Colgate, Northwestern never considered her a transfer. As a result, she received full credit for her courses at Colgate. Always file with the registrar for a "leave of absence," not a permanent parting. Otherwise, the situation can become much more complicated, and in order to transfer back, you will have to reapply as a new student. (See the section **Until We Meet Again,** in Chapter 4.)

Although transferring back is not a common practice, transferring *again* certainly is. In fact, it can become addictive. We spoke to one student who had switched schools seven times. Some people attribute moving around a lot to indecision. Others like Rachel Sargent, who went from the University of Colorado to SUNY Albany to Syracuse to Brown, says, "I'm a little worried about getting bored." Whatever your reasons, transferring more than once is probably not a good idea. You often lose credit. Friendships generally suffer. And in the long run, graduate schools and employers may consider you fickle.

9. *Be Patient*

It's obvious but forgettable advice. And even if you don't want to hear it, you know that all adjustment really takes is time. You thoroughly researched this school, so you know exactly why it's more right for you than where you were. You got in, so you belong.

BEYOND THE SIX-STEP PLAN: OTHER OPTIONS

- What if I don't get accepted as a transfer?
- What if I transferred and a year later I'm still miserable?
- What if after reading through all the difficulties of switching schools, I decide transferring is not for me?

You have other options.

But before you decide what to do next, find out what went wrong. If you were rejected as a transfer applicant, call the admissions office and ask why. You have nothing to lose by asking. And an objective evaluation of your strengths and weaknesses will be extremely helpful if you decide to reapply later. If you transferred already and the move has not improved your situation, take another look at the final questionnaire in Chapter 1. What do you hope to get out of college? Before you decide to transfer again, make a very specific list of your future goals.

You may have realized by now that the **Six-Step Plan** is not just for transferring. It is a useful way of approaching any major life move. Evaluating your situation, consulting family and friends, researching, acting on your decision, and reorienting your lifestyle are commonsense steps in any plan. When taking advantage of other options, don't forget to apply the **Six-Step Plan.** Most important, use Chapter 1 to make a full assessment of your current feelings. And be sure to research thoroughly any program you choose. Although going abroad or taking time off may not be as significant as transferring, they still demand time, energy, and money.

Higher education does not only take place in the classroom. Spending a year abroad doing fieldwork or living on a kibbutz can be just as educational as going to college. There are myriad ways to learn, some more formal than others. For many students, the purpose of taking time out from intensive study is to gain perspective on education itself, as well as to clarify one's goals for the future. We've compiled the following list of experiences for people who are looking for a change of pace.

Almost Transferring

Visiting student programs allow you to try something completely new by spending a year or semester at another school. It is a great opportunity to sample another college's classes, professors, facilities, and social life. Visiting is usually the most productive when you're a guest at a school very different from your own. Students often go from co-ed to single-sex, integrated to all-black, or southern to northern colleges. One semester in a radically new environment may be all the change you need.

Or you can attend a specialized school. Tracey Lord knew immediately that she wanted to leave Skidmore. But because she couldn't transfer after only one semester, she enrolled in the Eugene O'Neill Theater Institute. There Tracey was completely immersed in theater. In addition to acting, she designed costumes, wrote scripts, and directed plays. "It was one of the most intense experiences of my life. I loved it." She received full credit for the semester and a great deal of training. Your school should have an office with an extensive list of visiting opportunities. If not, look into fine arts academies and call the school you want to attend.

Formal programs are not the only way to visit. Eve Henderson wasn't sure what to do with her life when she left Kenyon her sophomore year. She eventually decided to move to

Amherst because she could live with friends. While there, Eve enrolled in classes at the University of Massachusetts, as part of their continuing education division and at Hampshire as a "special student." Although it was not an official visit, Eve paid for individual courses and did earn credit. She later transferred to the New School for Social Research.

The Love Boats

Semester At Sea and Sea Semester are not the same program, but both offer a way to study while sailing around the world.

The former is based at the University of Pittsburgh, and takes 500 students and two dozen professors around the globe each term. Students can select from over sixty courses, all of which have an international focus. Most colleges recognize the Semester At Sea program and will grant full academic credit. For information, write to Semester at Sea, Forbes Quad, University of Pittsburgh, PA 15620.

Sea Semester is a similar, but more competitive, program with a curriculum geared specifically toward nautical science. Prerequisites include courses in college-level math and lab science, and all majors are considered. The first half of the term is spent ashore in labs and classes. The remaining "sea component" is completed aboard a research vessel that cruises the East Coast for six weeks. Students from affiliated colleges can apply directly from their schools. All others must go through the office at Boston University. Write to Sea Education Association, P.O. Box 6, Woods Hole, MA 02543.

Study Abroad

An easy way to change your environment without changing your school is studying abroad. "In 1986 over half a million Americans attended school in a foreign country," according to *The Insider's Guide to Foreign Study* by Benedict Leerburger (Reading, MA: Addison-Wesley, 1988). This book is an extensive reference of over 400 accredited courses in 56 countries. It describes the classes, explains how to apply, and outlines the costs involved. The *Insider's Guide* is a good place to start looking if you still want an academic experience, just somewhere else, for a while.

Another excellent source on foreign programs is *Work, Study, Travel Abroad* published by the Council on International Educational Exchange (New York, NY: St. Martin's Press,

1990). It is a country-by-country guide to university-sponsored programs. Included is information about grants, scholarships, exchange programs, and teaching opportunities all over the world. The foreign studies office of your school should have a copy, as well as their own brochures and sources. Consult them first to see if you must go on an official program in order to receive credit. Many schools allow you to enroll directly at the foreign institution or with another university program.

Employment

Finding employment is easy. Finding interesting employment is not so easy, but it can be done. The best way to begin your job search is to read Richard Bolles' classic *What Color Is Your Parachute?* (Berkeley, CA: Ten Speed Press, 1989). He calls it a practical manual for job hunters and career changers, and it is about finding out what you like to do. Bolles includes countless references and resources, and helps you rigorously and honestly assess yourself: what skills you most enjoy using, where, and how.

One route to meaningful employment is the Venture program. The mission of the program is to place students into full-time, paid, temporary employment across the nation. There are no requirements and no credit is granted. About 400 students use the service annually in jobs ranging from innkeeping on Whidbey Island in Washington State to teaching sign language to gorillas in Washington, D.C. Venture is available to students enrolled at Brown, Bates, Colgate, Cornell, Northwestern, Skidmore, University of Chicago, Vassar, Wesleyan, and William & Mary universities.

Another source to consider is the *Summer Employment Directory of the United States,* edited by Pat Beusterien (Cincinnati, OH: Writer's Digest Books, 1989), which contains over 50,000 listings catalogued by state. The directory is updated annually and covers among other things, openings working for the federal government, teaching tennis at resorts, and managing summer theater.

Also check out *Work Your Way Around the World* by Susan Griffith (Oxford: Vacation World, 1989). In addition to information about how to find temporary jobs and obtain work permits, she includes profiles of other work-travelers' experiences. Some of the most interesting tips are on how to travel free by "working a passage." Cruise ships, vehicle-delivery companies, and air couriers all provide temporary mobile employment. As long as it's in another country, even the most menial work can be more meaningful.

And, of course, you can always wait tables. But if you think you might ever return to academia, it will be to your advantage to have spent your time off doing something intellectually fulfilling, socially redeeming, or at least related to your future career. There are innumerable exciting opportunities, so enjoy working before you have to get serious and find a "real job."

Volunteer Opportunities

Depending on your economic flexibility, you can use your time off to work as a volunteer for an endless array of national and international organizations. Overseas relief agencies, women's shelters, and soup kitchens are in desperate need of volunteers. Although charitable groups don't always have structured internships, if you tell them you're willing to work without wages, they will create a position. They may even be able to provide housing. The best part is you don't have to be qualified, and through volunteering you can gain invaluable experience that may later lead to paid employment.

If you're willing to break even, Lauren Tarshis's book *Taking Off: Extraordinary Ways to Spend Your First Year Out of College* (New York: Fireside Press, 1989) is a good resource. Nearly all of the experiences she includes do offer at least some kind of financial support. They range from going on archeological digs to teaching English in Asia to building houses for the poor. Tarshis also gives information about working at a summer camp, on a Native American reservation, or in a national park.

FINALLY

Wherever you do go, you will have to readjust. But it can be much easier than you think. As long as you plan ahead, aren't shy, get involved, explore, know your surroundings, don't depend on orientation programs, take advantage, go back to visit, and be patient, everything will work out fine.

Most of all, congratulate yourself. You've made a difficult decision and deserve lots of praise.

MICKEY MCDONALD
Boston University–Broward Community College–University of Northern Colorado–Florida State

"Looking back, I realize I should have taken a year off between high school and college." Instead, Mickey went directly to college and ended up transferring three times.

Mickey's parents wanted him to attend college directly from high school, and it was *"easier to go than figure out what to do with my life."* After attending a small private high school in Florida, he was ready to try a large, city school. Since many of his friends were going to college in Boston, Mickey decided to enroll at Boston University.

But bigger turned out not to be better. He felt overwhelmed by the number of students. *"B.U. was a sea of people. It was nothing like a college, just a city. There were four people with my first, last, and middle name."* He hated living in the all-male dorm, which he described as an *"unnatural environment."* The atmosphere was not conducive to meeting people.

From the first semester he considered dropping out, but it seemed easier to stay for the full year. The weather in Boston was *"too damn cold,"* and he found the frequent rain depressing. Academically he *"coasted"* through school, getting As in courses he liked and failing the rest. *"I didn't go to class very often and there were several courses I never completed,"* Mickey says. By March he decided that staying at B.U. would be a mistake. *"I felt like a leech. My parents were paying $18,000, and I wasn't doing any of the work."* He left with eleven credits.

His father was very upset at the decision and was worried that if Mickey didn't continue college, then he would never finish. His mother was more supportive and encouraged him to come back to Florida and start working. *"I flopped around a lot. I waited tables and saw the spectrum of people who don't go to college."* So, the next semester Mickey started taking courses at Broward Community College, just to *"keep in touch with going to school."* He did well in his music classes but didn't like any of the general education requirements. By the second semester he only registered part time for voice and piano. It was like *"taking private lessons through the college."* But Mickey never felt very connected to the school. Most of the students were older and going back to school, or young people *"not all that interested in school, but appeasing their parents."*

Then, in July of 1988, Mickey wanted a change of pace and felt he "needed to be in the mountains." He moved to Boulder, Colorado, that summer and worked in a resort. There he hung around a lot of people "with very few interests other than skiing." Although he enjoyed working, Mickey missed studying music.

"I think it's very important to respect the people who are teaching you. And I've always sort of felt that anyone could teach English. But music teachers have talent—something not everyone has." Mickey applied to the University of Northern Colorado in the fall, was accepted, and enrolled as a major in Voice. He decided to devote himself seriously to music. In addition to music theory and literature, he was required to take general education courses which he described as "a nice break." He did well academically and raised his grade point average considerably from what it was at B.U. But although Mickey liked the Music Department and the university, he felt he wasn't getting his "money's worth." "I was paying out-of-state tuition and it would have taken me forever to qualify for residency."

Mickey considered finishing the year but was worried about transfer credit problems. His parents suggested that he apply to Florida State where he could pay in-state tuition and continue studying music. His professors at the University of Northern Colorado wanted him to stay; the school even offered him a scholarship. But it wasn't enough money, and Mickey was ready to go back to Florida.

Florida State automatically gives all transfer students first-year status and requires that they take CLEP examinations. At the end of the first year, the university reevaluates students' records and adjusts their standing accordingly. Although Florida State has tentatively accepted thirty-eight of Mickey's credits, he won't know how much of his credit "officially transferred" until next spring. His biggest disappointment was losing all the credit he had earned in high school. "Suddenly all of my APs and achievements don't count. I have to repeat everything by taking Florida's exams."

Mickey admits that "being brand new" and constantly readjusting to different schools can be difficult. "But it's also neat, because you don't know what to expect." His friends think he's "nuts" for jumping around so much, but Mickey has thoroughly enjoyed his nomadic lifestyle.

When asked if there were any school he would have stayed at for four years, he said "Not in the beginning. I wasn't in the mind-set to do school at that point." At Florida State, Mickey will have the advantages of a small music school within a large state university. He's even thinking about enrolling in their five-year Master's program. Mickey's hoping this will be the school to grant his degree, and feels he's finally ready to stop moving and "settle into one thing and do it well."

Chapter 7

No Strings Attached (Transferring from a Junior College to a Four-Year School)

Within ten years there will be more people of color than caucasians in California. The entire University of California system has a clear-cut responsibility to get minorities into higher education.
—Donna Mekis, currently writing a dissertation on transfer rates between CA community and state schools

Most students who graduate from high school aren't ready to spend another four years going to class. Nor are their parents prepared to pay up to $80,000 for a bachelor's degree. Junior and community colleges provide a "no strings attached" alternative to a full-fledged four-year relationship. With a mere two-year commitment you can gain technical or vocational training, while you decide whether or not to transfer and complete your bachelor's degree.

Over half of all college freshmen attend two-year schools.[1] They are both cheaper and smaller than four-year schools and usually within commuting distance. Because their faculty is

1. Dale Parnell, *The Neglected Majority* (Washington, D.C.: Community College Press, 1986, p. 3).

dedicated to teaching and not research, junior colleges can give students personal attention. Also, most two-year colleges have **Open Admissions** policies and will admit all students with a high school diploma or its equivalent. With **Strategic Financial Planning** everyone has an opportunity to enroll in a two-year program with the possibility of later transferring to a competitive four-year school.

Although some junior colleges (JCs) are strictly technical or vocational schools, most award the **Associate of Arts** Degree (AA) as well. With this degree, a student can transfer directly to a four-year school. In fact, most community colleges have agreements with four-year schools allowing students with the AA to transfer smoothly. According to the American Association of Community and Junior Colleges (AACJC), one third of all JC students enroll primarily to transfer. **Admissions standards at four-year schools are often much less competitive for community college graduates than for traditional high school applicants.**

This chapter is for high school students considering the junior college alternative, JC students contemplating transfer, and others who are in the midst of the process. The information we have provided for JC students who want to transfer to a four-year school should give high school students a better sense of the advantages and disadvantages of attending a junior college.

DON'T CALL ME JUNIOR

There is no difference between a junior and a community college. Originally, all two-year schools were labeled "junior" colleges to distinguish them from "senior" institutions. In the 1960s the term "community college" became popular, and old schools started changing their names. Today the two names are used interchangeably, and many community colleges are actually four-year schools.

"Two-year college" is the commonly used term for institutions which grant associate degrees, but should not be taken literally in all cases. Some programs may be completed in as little as one year while others require three. Since so many JC students go to school part time, earning an AA could take much longer. When we refer to a junior, JC, community, or two-year college, we mean a school that grants the associate degree rather than, or in addition to, the bachelor's.

STRATEGIC FINANCIAL PLANNING

Josie Willard's parents did not support her decision to go to college. The only way she could continue her education was if she could find a way to earn the money herself. Josie used her savings from summer jobs to enroll at Grand Rapids Junior College during her senior year in high school. She stayed there for three years, alternately working and taking part-time course loads. After completing her AA she transferred to Michigan State, where she took out a Guaranteed Student Loan to pay for the last two years.

For many students like Josie, the junior college alternative is the only way to get a university degree. For a full discussion of strategic financial planning, see Chapter 2.

MAKING A GOOD IMPRESSION

Attending a two-year school is also a good way to strengthen your academic record. Tara McBride had a terrible senior year of high school. "I got mono and was really sick during my SATs." Obviously she did not perform to her potential, so she took a year off before going to college. While living at home, she worked and took courses part time at Ramapo Community College. "The break was really good for me. I did well on my own and got a feeling for what college was like." Now Tara is excited about going to college full time at Pine Manor next year. If you do take time off, admissions officers want to see that you've been productive. Doing well at a JC is a great way to compensate for a poor high school transcript.

Or you may just need time to get disciplined. Brad Hill's parents didn't think he was ready for college, so even though he was accepted at Syracuse, his first choice, he went to Dean Junior College in Massachusetts. "They wanted me to perform well. They thought I would get lost and distracted at such a big school." At Dean, Brad worked hard and learned how to schedule his time. He studied marketing and administration and after two years transferred into Syracuse's Business School. Many students successfully use junior colleges to prepare themselves for the rigor of a four-year school.

Specialized Schools

Specialized schools are not traditionally thought of as junior or community colleges. Yet art, architecture, and dramatic academies provide excellent two-year training for students who plan to attend a four-year college. This option is important for students who may not be ready to give up the security of a college degree for the unpredictable life of an actor. The American Academy of Dramatic Arts offers an AA for students who complete their two-year program, but admission to the second and third years is by invitation, so students who are not allowed back can transfer. Students who are invited back for the third year become automatic members of the Academy Company; they may never need to pursue a bachelor's degree. If you have artistic talent, you should certainly consider the advantages of a two-year specialized school.

ARTICULATION AGREEMENTS

A formal accord between a community college and a four-year school is called an **articulation agreement.** This agreement states exactly which courses transfer from one institution to another. A copy of all articulation agreements is available in the transfer office of the junior or senior college. Most JCs have articulation agreements with state universities, but recently more and more private four-year schools have begun establishing connections with JCs. In 1989, the National Project on Community College Transfer began a half-million-dollar effort to increase the number of students who transfer from two- to four-year colleges.[2] Now articulation agreements exist between Vassar, Smith, Bucknell, Lewis & Clark, Hamilton, and Agnes Scott and local junior and community colleges. Many other public and private four-year schools make a special effort to enroll transfers from junior and community colleges.

2. *The New York Times,* March 15, 1989.

AUTOMATIC TRANSFER

In fact, many junior and community colleges offer **automatic transfer** programs. These arrangements allow a graduate with an AA in a transfer program to move directly to a four-year college. Students do have to go through some admissions process, but it is usually just a formality. For instance, any student who earns an AA from a Florida community college is guaranteed admission in the Florida State University system.

CHOOSING A JUNIOR COLLEGE

It is easier to transfer from some junior and community colleges than others. Choosing a good school is obviously an important step in planning your educational career. *Peterson's Guide to Two-Year Colleges* is a helpful resource in finding such a school. There are a great variety of two-year colleges: technical, religious, public, private, and vocational. But choosing one can be much more difficult than selecting a four-year school because JC reputations are not as widely known.

You should begin your research by checking a college's **accreditation.** Given the wide range of JCs that exist, it is important to make sure that the school you choose meets certain national criteria. There are several regional accrediting agencies recognized by the Department of Education which evaluate schools in this country. The purpose of accreditation is to provide reliable assurance of the quality of graduates for other schools and employers. Any college to which you apply as a transfer will check your school's accreditation.

Colleges generally state their accreditation in brochures. Since most two-year college guidebooks only include accredited institutions, it is useful to start your search by reading their profiles.

Then investigate whether the college has articulation agreements with senior institutions. Find out about policies regarding automatic admissions. If your school has a formal accord, you may be able to avoid the uncertainty of reapplying and the angst of arranging transfer credit.

But in order to transfer successfully without articulation agreements, it is vital that you choose a two-year school that is respected. Informal connections between schools are very important and many JCs are **feeder schools** to four-year colleges. This means that the admissions office of the four-year college is familiar with the JC's curriculum, faculty, and the quality of its students. A long and solid transfer history between schools will be to your advantage when reapplying.

Transfer Tracks

If you are planning to transfer, choose a school with a "university-parallel" program, equivalent to the first two years of a bachelor's degree. These programs fulfill general education requirements and often do not lead to an AA. It is not necessary to earn an associate's degree in order to transfer; however, some four-year colleges strongly recommend that you do so. What is most important is that you design a course of study that is transferable. The curricular track you eventually choose must correspond to your transfer school's admissions and degree requirements.

Also look for schools with transfer offices and transfer counselors. Find out how much of the college's resources are devoted to helping students continue their education. Many schools have transfer centers where guidance and information about reapplying is easily accessible. Some offer computer programs and video libraries that will help you pick a target school. A counselor can tell you about special scholarships for transfers (including Phi Theta Kappa) and useful honors programs within the school. Almost all JCs have some program of advanced study. Even if it's informal, you should take advantage of your school's honors curriculum.

MAKING THE COMMITMENT
The Six-Step Plan for JC Transfers

An associate's degree is a valuable credential, but the economic benefits it offers are limited. By transferring, every student can obtain a bachelor's degree. In a recent year, 35,000 students from California community colleges transferred to senior schools in the California State and University of California systems.[3] Of course, the earlier you think about transferring, the more successful you will be, but even students who are about to graduate can transfer to a competitive four-year school.

All of the information and advice throughout this book applies to your situation. Yet there are issues that concern JC students in particular. Below is a summary of the **Six-Step Plan,** with additional information for two-year college transfers.

1. *Reevaluation*

The shift from a two-year college to a four-year one is a difficult one, so it is best to use your experience at a JC to figure out exactly what you are looking for in another school. Do you like the environment of a commuter college or do you feel you are missing the community of a residential campus? Do you like small classes or do larger lectures excite you? Use the questionnaires in Chapter 1 to help you pin down your feelings.

A very important part of reevaluation is understanding what you hope to gain out of higher education. Remember that most JC graduates do not continue their studies beyond the associate degree. Why do you want to transfer? What are your career goals and how will a bachelor's degree help you meet them?

As you proceed with reapplying, it will be important to appreciate what you have gotten out of the junior college experience. How has it changed the way you view the world? How have you grown since high school?

Even if you loved your JC experience, it is still the end of a relationship. Try making a list of the good and bad experiences

---

3. Arthur Cohen et al., *The Collegiate Function of Community Colleges* (San Francisco: Jossey-Bass, 1987).

of the last two years; it will give you a new perspective on your situation and help you plot a course for the future.

2. *Renegotiation*

Because most four-year colleges are more expensive than JCs, your parents may not be pleased by your decision to transfer. They may encourage you to find a job or get married, so it is doubly important that you have concrete reasons for pursuing a bachelor's degree. Keep in mind that the costs of going to a four-year college include not only tuition but room and board. While you may not have needed financial aid as a JC student, it may be important to apply for aid when you transfer. Both state and private colleges offer need-based scholarships, so see Chapter 2 for information about applying.[4]

Since many of your friends will directly enter the job market, you may feel very alone in your decision to transfer. But don't let peer pressure—or lack of peer support—change your mind. Remember that you will make many new friends at college, and you can always keep in touch with old ones.

3. *Research*

It is interesting that JC graduates rarely use the "reach or fall" plan when applying to transfer. They have clearly learned something that most high school students haven't. But because junior college life tends to be so different from four-year college life, extensive research is especially important.

It is time for you to decide what to study as a major. If you were pursuing a General Education degree, then you must focus your interests into one subject. Many four-year colleges will offer classes in subjects that do not even exist in JC curricula. Most four-year colleges have a **liberal arts** focus. Liberal arts courses are intended to provide chiefly general knowledge and to develop critical reasoning; they include study in the Humanities, Social Sciences, Physical and Life Sciences, and the Fine Arts.

---

4. As a matter of fact, many students who qualify for aid at state universities never ask for the money, according to a spokesperson for the American Association of Community and Junior Colleges.

The **Humanities** include:
- art history
- classics
- comparative literature
- English literature
- foreign languages
- philosophy

The **Social Sciences** include:
- anthropology
- economics
- ethnic studies (African-American, Asian-American, etc.)
- history
- political science
- psychology
- sociology

The **Physical and Life Sciences** include:
- astronomy
- biology
- botany
- chemistry
- computer science
- geology
- linguistics
- math
- neurology
- physics
- zoology

The **Fine Arts** include:
- dance
- drawing
- music
- painting
- sculpture
- theater

In addition to these areas there are a whole range of interdisciplinary courses, such as International Relations, Urban Studies, and Religious Studies. There are also the applied fields of Education, Health, and Engineering.

None of these majors leads directly to a specific job. All of them will, however, teach you to think critically. And since they all develop similar analytical capacities, you will be able to apply your skills to any career.

Try to discover what fields interest you the most. Which subjects sound the most exciting4 What issues do you want to spend a lot of time thinking about? Consider all your options before you declare a major. You may find after one year at a senior college that you would like to spend the rest of your life studying. There are always spaces for interested students in graduate programs, and there is a growing need for professors with doctorates. You may even want to consider a career as a university professor.

In addition to focusing your course of study, you will also want to find a school that is just right for you. Your reevaluation should help you in that search.

Differences Between a Typical Junior College and a Four-Year School

Junior College	Senior College
free to moderately expensive	moderate to very expensive
most students commute	most students live in dormitories or in off-campus apartments
easy to open admissions	competitive to very competitive admissions
enrollment usually under 3,000	enrollment usually over 3,000
specializing in technical, vocational, and general ed.	specializing in liberal arts
most instructors have Master's degrees	most instructors have doctoral degrees
professors teach classes	professors lecture and research, graduate students run sections
many part-time students	few part-time students

Obviously all four-year institutions are different. State universities will be much larger than private undergraduate colleges. They will have bigger classes, probably offer more activities, and have greater facilities. If you have enjoyed the advantages of a small two-year school, consider applying to a private college.

Many JC students assume that they cannot afford tuition at a private college, but don't realize that they may be eligible for financial aid. Don't be dissuaded by prestigious reputations, either. If you have what it takes to succeed in college, you might as well aim for the best. Kumar Pandey came from a college in Nepal to study in the United States. He lived with his brother in Florida and enrolled at Tallahassee Community College. There he studied very hard, improved his English, and after completing his degree, applied to several very competitive colleges. Kumar is now a junior at Brown University.

In addition, many private schools make a special effort to recruit JC graduates. When you research, keep in mind that your background may give you a distinct advantage over other applicants.

4. *Reapplication*

As soon as you are considering transferring, tell your college guidance counselor. He or she may arrange for you to see special transfer counselors, meet with university representatives, and take trips to nearby universities. Plus, he or she can provide you with important transfer information and tell you about on-campus lectures by university professors.

The students who transfer most successfully are those who participate fully in their junior college experience.[5] So, take advantage of student clubs, college forums, and on-campus jobs to meet friends and get the most out of your undergraduate years.

All of the general guidelines outlined in Chapter 4 for the reapplication procedure apply to JC students. Good recommendations are extremely important because admissions officers need to make sure that you can handle the increased workload of a four-year school. Even if it is not required, we strongly recommend that you have an interview. Meeting in person will allow you the opportunity to ask extensive questions about the school's academic policies, particularly transfer credit.

5. Cohen et al., *The Collegiate Function of Community Colleges.*

Transfer Credit

The largest difference between transferring from a JC as opposed to a four-year school is arranging transfer credit. Many students mistakenly think that it is easier to transfer from a four- rather than a two-year school. Ned Conner wasn't sure what he wanted from college, so he decided to go to U.C. Santa Barbara for a general liberal arts background. After two years he knew he wanted to transfer to a technical school. He's now happy at the California Polytechnic Institute, but says, "I should have gone to a California JC. As it was, I got screwed in units and only four classes transferred." If you apply to an institution that has an articulation agreement with your junior college, all of your courses should transfer without delay.

Many states have **common course numbering systems,** which also make arranging transfer credit much easier. For example, first-year English is numbered 101 at both the state university and all state community colleges. Nevertheless, a common numbering system can be deceptive. A university may not grant full credit for particular community college courses, so it is important to examine all articulation agreements closely.

If your JC does not have an articulation agreement with the school to which you want to transfer, arranging credit will be more difficult. Four-year private colleges, sometimes suspicious of AA degrees, will thoroughly investigate the content and level of your courses before granting credit. Keep in mind that four-year liberal arts colleges expect you to have taken substantive *liberal arts* classes. Specialized or vocational courses in business or engineering will not transfer to a liberal arts school. Students are often surprised to find that their rigorous course in marketing won't count toward their degree while an introductory piano class will. Most JCs have General Education majors that include courses in all the disciplines of the liberal arts. General Ed. courses should transfer easily. Other four-year schools, such as business or engineering colleges, prefer students who have demonstrated a clear focus in their area of study and will only award credit for classes similar to ones offered by the four-year school. If you are planning to follow a vocational track, concentrate your study in order to earn *transferable* credit.

When planning your course schedule:

- Consult a transfer counselor
- Take solid courses in your intended major

- If you are planning on transferring to a liberal arts college, avoid specialized, vocational, or technical courses

- Enroll in honors programs

- If you know where you want to transfer, call that school and find out what courses will receive credit.

If you are trying to transfer to a school with which your JC doesn't have an articulation agreement, you may need to convince the admissions office that your college is a respected institution. Send a copy of an articulation agreement your school has with another four-year college. This will illustrate that your JC is reputable and well regarded by other four-year institutions.

But no matter where you are applying, it is important to send the Transfer Credit Packet described in Chapter 4. This includes your Suggested Course Equivalency Chart, a Projected Academic Program, all syllabi for classes in dispute, and the most recent copy of your school's course catalogue.

CLEP

The College Board offers a series of general and subject examinations for college applicants who have gained learning in nontraditional ways. College Level Entrance Placement (CLEP) exams are usually taken by students who have been out of school for many years, but JC students may find them useful as well. To find out test dates and locations, consult a counselor at your school.

Before taking the test, however, check with the new school and *your academic department* to make sure that credit or placement is given for CLEP exams. When Leslie Sickterman applied to transfer as an English major, the University of Michigan assured her that they would accept her CLEP scores. After enrolling, however, she learned that English is the only department that doesn't recognize equivalency exams. She ended up going to summer school to make up the credit. Nevertheless, equivalency tests can be a good way to earn credit, so find out about specific transfer policies before you apply.

NCAA Regulations

Two-year college transfers to a Division I or II school, like other transfers, must complete a one-year residence requirement before being allowed to play. Again there are many exceptions to this rule. Where it says JC below, it means specifically two-year colleges.

A. If before enrolling in a JC you met the requirements for academic eligibility (see C below), you may play immediately at a Division I school. You must have spent at least 2 semesters at the JC, earned a minimum of 24 semester hours (or 36 quarter hours) of transferable credit, and had a GPA of 2.0 or better.

B. If before enrolling in the JC you did not meet the requirements for academic eligibility, you may play immediately as long as you have completed a minimum of 48 semester hours (or 72 quarter hours) of transferable credit, with a GPA of 2.0.

C. To meet the requirements for academic eligibility (qualifier status), you must have graduated high school with a GPA of 2.0 and achieved a 700 combined score on the SAT or a 15 composite score on the ACT. You must also have completed in high school a "core curriculum" of eleven academic courses including: three years of English, two years of math, two years of social science, and two years of natural or physical science.

D. In order to play immediately at a Division II school, you do not need to have qualifier status. But you must have graduated from the JC or earned a minimum of 24 semester hours (or 36 quarter hours) of transferable credit, with a GPA of 2.0.

E. Mid-year transfers are not eligible to compete immediately if they played at a JC in that same academic year.

F. If you have attended more than one JC, you may combine all of your credits in order to satisfy the above requirements.

5. *Revision*
The essay is always important, but it is doubly so for applicants from junior colleges. Admissions officers will be reading your essay in order to judge the level of your writing ability. Because junior colleges have minimum admissions standards, it is crucial that you demonstrate good writing. In Chapter 5 we warned other transfers not to send unsolicited writing samples to the admissions office. But if you have a piece of creative or critical writing that demonstrates your ability, by all means

send it. It can be an academic paper, an article, a short story, or poetry. Always make sure you have someone proofread your work for spelling and grammatical errors before you put it in the mail.

You don't need to spend as much time discussing your reasons for applying in the actual essay as other transfers do. Instead, you need to explain why you intend to pursue a bachelor's degree, why you chose to attend a junior college in the first place, and what you have gotten out of the junior college experience. If you went to a two-year college for financial reasons, be sure to mention that fact. And if you paid your own tuition, emphasize how that experience has made you a more mature and responsible individual.

Think of your essay as an argument and read the examples in Chapter 5 of deductive and inductive styles. It is still a love letter, and you have to convince an admissions office why they should want you at their school. Capitalize on what makes you different from other students. Prove to an admissions officer how you will contribute to the diversity of the school.

Feel free to discuss specific career goals in your essay. Link them to the school, showing how you expect to fulfill your aspirations there. And remember, a major purpose of your essay is to demonstrate your writing ability, so pick a topic with which you feel comfortable. Nevertheless, you do want to illustrate how attending a four-year college fits into your new vision of the future.

6. *Readjustment*

Despite the differences between a JC and a senior college, readjustment will probably be much easier for you than for other transfers. There is no reason why you should be doubting or rejecting your decision, and you should be comfortable in the knowledge that you completed your education at your last school. (You can't go back even if you wanted to.) Plus, you have all the excitement of starting completely anew. Still, adjusting to a new environment is never easy, and the nine suggestions listed in Chapter 6 should help ease the transition.

TRANSFER SHOCK

Be prepared for large differences in course work and academic rigor at the new school. JC transfers often experience what is known as "transfer shock." The first semester after transferring, their grades go down. Don't be alarmed, because your grades should return to your previous average by the second semester.[6] "Generally, JC students retain their relative scholastic standing after transfer. Those that were high stay high; those that were low stay low."[7]

Good study habits are an important part of making the transition from a junior to a senior college. Before you transfer, see if your JC offers any courses on study skills. Or you may be able to find such a course at your new school.

Living in a dorm, participating in school activities, and studying hard will help you get the most out of senior college life. During the early part of your transition, try to meet with an advisor or peer counselor as often as possible; you'll be less likely to fall behind. Always ask questions, and never lose the self-confidence that has brought you thus far.

ADDITIONAL INFORMATION ABOUT JUNIOR COLLEGES

4-2 and 4-2-4 Transferring

A number of students opt to transfer from a four-year program to a two-year program for financial or academic reasons. This is called **4-2 transferring** (not to be confused with **reverse transferring,** below). Readjustment to a junior college can be especially difficult because most are nonresidential and do not offer the same feeling of campus life found at a traditional school. If you are planning to 4-2 transfer, make sure you keep open the possibility of returning to your original school.

Students who do return to their original four-year college are called **4-2-4 transfers.** There are separate NCAA rules for 4-2-4 transfers, so contact the Legislative Services office (913-384-3220) or a coach at your school.

6. See Cohen et al., *The Collegiate Function of Community Colleges,* p. 156.

7. Robert Palinchak, *The Evolution of the Community College* (Princeton, NJ: Scarecrow Press, 1974), p. 82.

Reverse Transfer

Fifteen percent of all junior and community college students already have a bachelor's degree.[8] Many of these people have returned to school to acquire technical or job training, or to pick up a particular skill, such as typing. **Reverse transferring** is a basically simple task, which does not require arranging transfer credit or complicated application. If your bachelor's degree is not paying off in the job market, consider the advantages of taking free courses at a local community college.

CONCLUSION

Community colleges provide an excellent opportunity for students who have limited financial resources or who are not ready to make the commitment to spending four years in higher education. They are smaller and more intimate than most universities, and they are usually within commuting distance. Most important, community colleges are open to students of all educational backgrounds.

Transferring from a two-year to a four-year school is not always easy, but the advantages of pursuing a bachelor's degree are many. Because most JCs were originally intended to help students get a general education before attending a senior institution, they usually have transfer offices and special advisors to make transferring simple. If you need assistance in finding a school that will accept JC graduates, or have questions about your associate's degree, contact the American Association of Community and Junior Colleges in Washington, D.C.

---

8. According to Connie Odens, Vice-President of the American Association of Community and Junior Colleges.

JUAN VALDEZ
Foothill Junior College–
California Polytechnic State University

Juan Valdez enrolled at Foothill Junior College knowing he would later transfer. After high school, he wasn't sure exactly what he wanted to study so he decided to take general education courses at a local JC. He lived at home and worked part time. Going to a JC was an inexpensive way to experiment. He stayed at Foothill two years but did not earn an associate's degree. "I didn't see the point. To transfer, all I needed was a General Education certification."

Juan started researching transfer schools right after his first year. He had decided he wanted to study architecture—"I love art and drawing and also enjoy the math part of it." He was interested in California Polytechnic, known for its strong architecture and engineering programs. Since he had friends going there, he visited often. On one of his trips, Juan interviewed professors and fourth-year architecture students. He asked them detailed questions about courses, the department's philosophy, and admissions criteria. He also spoke to one of the school's guidance counselors in order to discuss exactly what classes he should take for his remaining year at Foothill. "It's a must to go to the university where you plan on transferring." Juan had no trouble with transferring credit. He even avoided chemistry, which his JC counselor had advised him to take but he found he didn't need for California Polytechnic.

Juan feels he didn't have to adjust to transferring at all. His classes have stayed small and he received a lot of one-to-one, teacher-student interaction at both schools. Having good friends from high school at Cal. Poly made meeting people easy. And he loves being in San Luis Obispo—"This area is absolutely beautiful."

Going from one quarter system to another was also a big plus. Being familiar with the system was definitely to his advantage. "Quarters go very fast. Before you know it, you have midterms. It was really hard for people used to semesters." Juan is majoring in City and Original Planning and hopes to pursue a career in "large-scale design."

In spite of his two years at Foothill, Juan still has to complete several upper-division general education courses. California Polytechnic has strict distribution requirements in the humanities for all graduates because they are "trying to form well-rounded students." Juan lives in an off-campus apartment and regularly attends summer school. Since he has to devote so much of his time during the year to architecture lab, he doesn't have room in his schedule for all the "general stuff." He doesn't mind spending summers fulfilling requirements and is "glad we've got all that incorporated into the curriculum."

Juan's parents were supportive throughout the transfer process and are very proud of his accomplishments. He believes that going to Foothill was a good experience but that only attending a junior college wouldn't have been enough. "In order to grow up and mature, you need to go away from home." Juan is planning to continue his study of architecture in graduate school sometime in the future.

Afterword

**If you bought this book because you just got into
the "wrong" school and think you might
want to transfer . . .**

Don't despair. There are many things you can do to turn the
"wrong" school into the right one, and if that doesn't work,
transferring will. In fact, you have a large advantage over
anyone who doesn't realize until after sophomore year that he
or she is miserable, because you can plan ahead. Below we have
included a list of tactics that will help you transfer smoothly.

In any case, don't spend your first week looking to see what's
wrong with the school. Search instead for what's good about it.
Try to find the most interesting people, the best classes, and the
most popular professors. If you start to feel truly homesick, go
back for a few days. The sense of security that comes from being
able to return home should make you feel less imprisoned.

If after several weeks you are sure that transferring is the
only solution, begin to make the necessary provisions. The
following is a list of strategies for getting ahead; the points
correspond to themes in each of the chapters, so use the chart
as a brief reference guide to the book.

The Plan Ahead Chart
If You Are Unhappy and Thinking about Transferring

Create the Perfect Transfer's Transcript

- Get **Good Grades**
- Take Solid **Liberal Arts** Courses
- Take Courses That Are **Easily Transferable**
- **Don't** Take Courses Pass/Fail
- **Stay Away from** Classes with Superficial-Sounding Names

Begin Researching

- Pick **Ten Things That Must Be True of Your Ideal School**
- Read **Secondary Sources**
- Read **Primary Sources**
  —most importantly, the **Course Catalogue**
  —school newspapers
- Find Out about **Housing, Orientation, Residency Requirements**
- Identify Your **Reasons for Leaving** and Your Valid and Compelling **Reasons for Applying**
- **Visit**
  —Interview students, faculty, and administrators
  —Meet with transfers
  —Consult coaches
  —Talk to students in your department or activity
- Find Out about **Transfer Credit** Policies
- Find Out about **Financial Aid, Deadlines, Mid-Year Application**
- Initiate **Correspondence with Faculty**

Make the Most of Your Year

- **Get Involved** in Your School (so that you can show you made the most of your time there)
- Meet with Advisors, Deans, and Counselors at Your Present School
- Investigate Other Options

GLOSSARY

AACJC: American Association of Community and Junior Colleges.

accreditation: A process by which colleges and universities are evaluated to determine whether they meet established standards of educational quality.

Advanced Placement examinations (AP): An exam, usually taken in high school, that allows students to receive credit for college-level courses.

articulation agreements: Stipulations between universities and junior/community colleges regarding transfer credit.

Associate of Arts (AA): A two-year general education degree.

Bachelor of Arts (BA): The baccalaureate degree, representing four years of study in the liberal arts.

College Level Examination Program (CLEP): A series of general and subject examinations for college applicants who have gained learning in nontraditional ways (i.e., independent reading, on-the-job training, or correspondence courses).

community college: Two- and four-year colleges started in the 1960s, whose express purpose was to create an equal opportunity for higher education for all Americans. They are less expensive and less competitive than other four-year colleges.

concurrent enrollment: Enrolling at two colleges at the same time. Most schools have policies restricting concurrent enrollment.

consortia: Cooperative associations of colleges and universities which give students the opportunity to use the libraries of or take courses at all member institutions.

conversion factor: The equation to convert credits from one school to another. Divide the total number of transferable credits by the total number of credits needed to graduate at first school and multiply by the total number of credits needed to graduate at new school. The product is the number of credits you will have upon entering new school.

Financial Aid Form (FAF): A financial information form submitted to the College Scholarship Service, which gives the colleges to which the student applies an evaluation of his or her actual need.

4-2 transferring: Going from a four-year college to a two-year college while still an undergraduate.

4-2-4 transferring: Going from a four-year college to a two-year college and then returning to a four-year school.

guest semester: see **visiting students program**

intercampus transferring (or intrauniversity transferring): Going from one campus to another within the same university, or transferring from one college to another on the same campus.

junior college: A public or private two-year college granting the Associate of Arts Degree.

mid-year admissions: The policy of accepting students for the spring semester. Most schools have two separate deadlines (fall and spring); others have only a fall deadline but will admit students for both the spring and fall semesters.

NCAA: National Collegiate Athletic Association.

need-blind admissions: The policy of accepting students without regard to financial need. In other words, the admissions office reviews an applicant's folder without examining his or her financial situation.

Open Admissions: A policy whereby a two-year college accepts all applicants who have a high school diploma or its equivalent.

Pell Grant: A federal aid program designed to provide financial assistance to full- or half-time students. Students and their families must meet certain financial criteria to receive grants, which can range from $214 to $2,200.

primary sources: Anything published by a school or any person directly affiliated with a school. A written primary source includes school newspapers, magazines, alumni publications, academic journals, and admissions brochures.

Projected Academic Program: A list of courses that you plan to take at your new school and the semesters in which you plan to take them. (See **Transfer Credit Packet.**)

"reach or fall" plan: The traditional approach to college applications in which one applies to many schools, including several "reaches" and "safety's."

reasons for applying: These are your reasons for chosing a particular school. In order to be *valid* they must be academic reasons, and in order to be *compelling* they must be specific and demonstrate exactly why you have chosen the school.

reasons for leaving: These are your personal reasons for deciding to transfer. They can range from academic and social problems to dissatisfaction with the weather.

residency requirement: The number of terms a student must spend at one school in order to earn a degree. Calculated in semesters, quarters, or credit hours.

reverse transferring: Enrolling in a junior college after receiving a bachelor's degree from a four-year school (not to be confused with **4-2 transferring**).

Rolling Admissions: A policy whereby a college gives an admissions decision as soon as possible after an application is completed. Applications are accepted throughout the year and there is no set notification deadline.

ROTC: Many colleges have units of the Reserve Officer's Training Corps that offer two- and four-year programs of military training culminating in an officer's commission. In some colleges, credit for courses can be applied toward a degree.

secondary sources: Any source not directly related to a school, such as magazine articles, guidance counselors, and college guidebooks.

The Six-Step Plan:
   Reevaluation: The first step to getting it right the second time. Extensive evaluation of yourself and your school.

   Renegotiation: Overcoming the obstacles of family, friends, and finances.

Research: The smart way to find a new school that is *just right* for you. Thorough investigation entails reading primary and secondary sources, visiting the campus, and asking specific questions. Intensive research will improve your essay, strengthen your overall application, heighten your performance in an admissions interview, and make readjustment easier.

Reapplication: The actual process of applying. Includes arranging transfer credit, securing recommendations, and having an interview.

Revision: Writing the transfer essay.

Readjustment: Settling into your new school.

Strategic Financial Planning: Enrolling in an inexpensive junior or state college for two years and then transferring to a more expensive four-year school.

Suggested Course Equivalency Chart: A list of all courses taken at one school and equivalent courses at another. Prepared by the student during reapplication in order to facilitate the arrangement of transfer credit. (See **Transfer Credit Packet.**)

target school: The school to which you want to transfer.

transcript: The official record of a student's academic performance.

transfer coordinator: Admissions officer responsible for handling transfer applications.

Transfer Credit Packet: All validation materials sent to the admissions office during the reapplication process. Includes Suggested Course Equivalency Chart, Projected Academic Program, course syllabi, and cover letter.

transfer student: A student who has attended another college for any period from a single term up to three years.

Transfer Students' Responsibilities and Rights: A statement adopted by the National Association of College Admissions Counselors to help all transfer students understand their responsibilities and rights during the admissions process.

transferable credits: Credits accepted by your transfer school that will count toward graduation.

validation materials: Written documentation of completed coursework used to obtain transfer credit (i.e., syllabi, course catalogues, and letters from professors).

visiting students program: A program which allows students to spend a semester or a year at another institution without transferring.

work-study program: A federally subsidized employment and study program. Students are paid an hourly rate in libraries and administrative offices to help pay their college expenses.

yield: The percentage of students who matriculate out of the total number of students who receive offers of admission.

APPENDIX: COLLEGE PROFILES

The following appendix contains information on over 100 colleges and universities in the United States that accept transfer students. Every school selected falls into at least one of three categories: those that accept the highest proportion of applicants, those that accept the highest number of applicants, and those that receive the greatest number of applications each year. Entries are arranged alphabetically.

Each profile indicates:

- The address, name of the Director of Admissions, and the phone number of the admissions office.
- The name of the transfer coordinator, if available.
- The average number of transfer applicants and those admitted each year, or the figures for the most recent academic year available.
- Whether or not a school has articulation agreements with local junior colleges.
- Whether or not on-campus housing is guaranteed for transfers and the cost of room and board.
- The cost of tuition.
- The minimum grade point average necessary for admission.
- The number of semesters or credit hours that must be completed in residence.

- Whether or not transfers are accepted mid-year.
- The deadlines for transfer application.
- Any additional information the school provided about transfer admission.

Tuition and housing information are for the academic year 1989–90. There is a general 10 percent increase in cost each year. Note that some schools include two tuition figures: one for in-state and one for out-of-state applicants.

Adelphi University

Ellen Hartigan
Dean of Admissions
Garden City, NY 11530
(516) 663-1100

Transfer Coordinator: Susan Weit

Transfer Applicants: 1100
Admitted: 850

Articulation Agreements: Yes

On-Campus Housing: Guaranteed
Room & Board: $4500

Tuition: $7350

Minimum Requirements: 2.5 GPA

Residency: 30 credits for students from 4-year colleges
56 credits for students from 2-year colleges

Mid-Year: Yes

Deadlines: Nov. 1 (Spring)
July 1 (Fall)

Additional Comments:
Adelphi University gives preference to nontraditional students. Almost half of its transfer students are enrolled part time. Adelphi will accept a maximum of 64 credits for transfers from two-year colleges and 90 for those from four-year schools. Over 50% of Adelphi's entering class is comprised of transfer students.

Alfred University

Michael McKeon
Admissions Director
Alfred, NY 14802
(607) 871-2111
(800) 541-9229

Transfer Applicants: Fall: 260, Spring: 52
Admitted: Fall: 142 (enrolled), Spring: 28 (enrolled)

Articulation Agreements: With approx. 30 junior colleges

On-Campus Housing: Guaranteed
Room & Board: $3420

Tuition: $11,900

Minimum Requirements: 2.5 GPA

Residency: 4 sems.

Mid-Year: Yes

Deadlines: Aug. 1 (Fall)
             Dec. 1 (Spring)

Additional Comments:
Alfred University will consider candidates with 2.0 GPAs in some circumstances. Transfer students are accepted for all classes.

Amherst College

Dean Linda Davis Taylor
Director of Admissions
Amherst, MA 01002
(413) 542-2328

Transfer Coordinator: Amy Johnson

Transfer Applicants: 250
Admitted: 25–30

Articulation Agreements: None

On-Campus Housing: Guaranteed (see below)
Room & Board: $4000

Tuition: $12,850

Minimum Requirements: 3.4 GPA

Residency: 4 sems.

Mid-Year: Yes

Deadlines: Feb. 1 (Fall)
Nov. 1 (Spring)

Additional Comments:
Amherst College gives first priority for transfers who are community college graduates, older students, and veterans. SATs and ACTs are not required for admission. No credit is given for engineering courses or math courses under calculus. There is no visiting students program, but Amherst participates in the 12 College Exchange. Housing is guaranteed except for married students with spouses or dependent children.

Antioch College

Stephanie Chapko
Dean of Admissions
Yellow Springs, OH 45387
(513) 767-6400

Transfer Applicants: 150
Admitted: 110

Articulation Agreements: None

On-Campus Housing: Guaranteed
Room & Board: $3400

Tuition: $11,200

Minimum Requirements: 2.5 GPA

Residency: 80 quarter credits

Mid-Year: Yes

Deadlines: Rolling Admissions but recommended dates are:
July 15 (Fall)
Nov. 15 (Winter)
Feb. 15 (Spring)

Additional Comments:
Antioch College reviews transfer and freshman applicants together. The admissions criteria are the same and the SAT is recommended but not required.

Babson College

Joseph Carver
Dean of Admissions
Babson Park, MA 02157
(617) 235-1200

Transfer Applicants: 250–275
Admitted: 100–125

Articulation Agreements: (see below)

On-Campus Housing: Not Guaranteed
Room & Board: $5500

Tuition: $11,000

Minimum Requirements: Average GPA is 3.2

Residency: 64 credit hours

Mid-Year: Yes

Deadlines: April 1 (Fall)
Nov. 1 (Spring)

Additional Comments:
Babson does not have formal articulation agreements with other colleges but does have "some clear understandings with some two-year colleges."

Barnard College

Christine Royer
Director of Admissions
3009 Broadway
New York, NY 10027-6598
(212) 280-2041

Transfer Applicants: 340
Admitted: 185

Articulation Agreements: None

On-Campus Housing: Guaranteed
Room & Board: $6198

Tuition: $13,000

Minimum Requirements: 3.5 GPA

Residency: 60 credits

Mid-Year: Yes

Deadlines: Rolling Admissions for Fall
Nov. (Spring)

Baylor University

Bobby Schrade
Director of School Relations
Waco, TX 76798
(817) 755-3435

Transfer Applicants: n/a
Admitted: 500

Articulation Agreements: Yes

On-Campus Housing: Not Guaranteed
Room & Board: $3400

Tuition: $4620

Minimum Requirements: 2.5 GPA (cumulative)

Residency: 4 sems.

Mid-Year: Yes

Deadlines: Rolling Admissions

Additional Comments:
Students applying to Baylor University must maintain a 2.5
GPA for the last semester preceding transfer.

Beloit College

Thomas Martin
Admissions Director
Beloit, WI 53511
(608) 365-3391

Transfer Coordinator: Frank V. Luvillo

Transfer Applicants: 100–125
Admitted: 50

Articulation Agreements: (see below)

On-Campus Housing: Guaranteed
Room & Board: $2688

Tuition: $10,778

Minimum Requirements: 2.7 GPA

Residency: 4 sems.

Mid-Year: Yes

Deadlines: May 1 (Fall)
              Dec. 15 (Spring)

Additional Comments:
Beloit College has articulation agreements with the University of Wisconsin at Rock Valley and Harper Junior College in Chicago.

Birmingham Southern College

Robert Dortch
Admissions Director
Birmingham, AL 35254
(205) 226-4686

Transfer Applicants: 150
Admitted: 100

Articulation Agreements: None

On-Campus Housing: Not Guaranteed
Room & Board: $3000

Tuition: $7500

Minimum Requirements: (see below)

Residency: 4 sems.

Mid-Year: Yes

Deadlines: June 1 (Fall)

Additional Comments:
Birmingham Southern College requires a 2.0 GPA and a combined SAT score of 800 or an ACT composite score of 19.

Boston College

Charles Nolan
Admissions Director
Chestnut Hill, MA 02167
(617) 552-3100

Transfer Coordinator: Matthew Fissinger

Transfer Applicants: Fall: 1600, Spring: 350
Admitted: Fall: 200–250, Spring: 40–60

Articulation Agreements: None

On-Campus Housing: Not Guaranteed
Room & Board: $5200

Tuition: $10,700

Minimum Requirements: 2.5 GPA

Residency: 4 sems.

Mid-Year: Yes, but not for freshmen

Deadlines: May 1 (Fall)
           Nov. 1 (Spring)

Bowdoin College

William R. Masson
Director of Admissions
Brunswick, ME 04001
(207) 725-3100

Transfer Coordinator: Sammie T. Robinson

Transfer Applicants: 75–100
Admitted: 7–9

Articulation Agreements: None

On-Campus Housing: Not Guaranteed
Room & Board: $4380

Tuition: $12,435

Minimum Requirements: 3.0 GPA

Residency: 4 sems.

Mid-Year: No

Deadlines: April 15 (Fall)

Brandeis University

Director of Admissions
Waltham, MA 02254
(617) 736-3500

Transfer Applicants: 350
Admitted: 125

Articulation Agreements: None

On-Campus Housing: Not Guaranteed
Room & Board: $5500

Tuition: $12,700

Minimum Requirements: Recommended 3.0 GPA

Residency: 4 sems.

Mid-Year: Yes

Deadlines: April 1 (Fall)
Dec. 1 (Spring)

Additional Comments:
Brandeis University has only 40–60 beds per year for transfer students.

Brown University

Eric Widmer
Dean of Admissions
Providence, RI 02912
(401) 863-2378

Transfer Applicants: 700–800
Admitted: 60–65

Articulation Agreements: None

On-Campus Housing: Guaranteed
Room & Board: $4300

Tuition: $13,375

Minimum Requirements: (see below)

Residency: 4 sems.

Mid-Year: Yes

Deadlines: April 1

Additional Comments:
Brown University operates on the block system: a semester's worth of credit is given for 3 to 5 classes. There are no minimum requirements for admission. Brown offers a combined five-year Bachelor of Arts and Bachelor of Science Degree. Transfers to this program must complete a minimum of three years in residence.

Bryn Mawr College

Elizabeth Vermey
Director of Admissions
Lewisburg, PA 17837
(717) 524-1101

Transfer Applicants: 70–100
Admitted: 20–30

Articulation Agreements: None

On-Campus Housing: Guaranteed
Room & Board: $5100

Tuition: $12,500

Minimum Requirements: 3.0 GPA

Residency: 4 sems.

Mid-Year: On a space-available basis

Deadlines: March 15 (Fall)
Nov. 1 (Spring)

Bucknell University

Richard Skelton
Dean of Admissions
Lewisburg, PA 17837
(717) 524-1101

Transfer Applicants: Fall: 150, Spring: 40
Admitted: Fall: 68, Spring: 26

Articulation Agreements: None

On-Campus Housing: Not Guaranteed
Room & Board: $3475

Tuition: $13,725

Minimum Requirements: 2.5 GPA

Residency: 3 sems. (48 sem. hours)

Mid-Year: Yes

Deadlines: April 1 (Fall)
Dec. 1 (Spring)

Additional Comments:
A student may transfer to Bucknell with no less than 15 and no more than 80 semester hours of college work. Traditionally 30% of Bucknell's incoming transfer students are from two-year colleges. An AA is not required but candidates are strongly encouraged to complete their degree. There is usually more room available for rising juniors than there is for rising sophomores.

California Institute of Technology

Director of Admissions
Pasadena, CA 91125
(818) 356-6341

Transfer Applicants: 80
Admitted: 8–10

Articulation Agreements: None

On-Campus Housing: Not Guaranteed and depends on the size of the freshman class

Room & Board: $3947

Tuition: $12,760

Minimum Requirements: 3.0 GPA

Residency: (see below)

Mid-Year: No

Deadlines: April 1 (Fall)

Additional Comments:
At the California Institute of Technology residency is finished when "the prescribed work in one of the options is completed, with a passing grade in each required subject." In addition to a 3.0 GPA the school requires the SAT, one year of calculus, and one year of calculus-based physics.

Carnegie Mellon University

Michael Steidel
Director of Admissions
Pittsburgh, PA 15213
(412) 578-2082

Transfer Applicants: 445
Admitted: 172

Articulation Agreements: None

On-Campus Housing: Not Guaranteed
Room & Board: $4320

Tuition: $13,000

Minimum Requirements: Same as freshman applicants

Residency: 2 years

Mid-Year: On a space-available basis

Deadlines: April 1 (Fall)
Nov. 1 (Spring)

Case Western Reserve

Jean A. Scott
Dean of Admissions
Cleveland, OH 44106
(800) 321-6984

Transfer Coordinator: Jamie Hobba

Transfer Applicants: 276
Admitted: 172

Articulation Agreements: (see below)

On-Campus Housing: Not Guaranteed (85% of students do receive housing)

Room & Board: $4300

Tuition: $11,000

Minimum Requirements: (see below)

Residency: 60 credit hours

Mid-Year: Yes

Deadlines: June 30 (Fall)
            Nov. 15 (Spring)

Additional Comments:
The suggested GPA for applicants is 3.0, and an interview is recommended. The combined average SAT score of incoming freshmen is 1162; the average ACT composite, 27. Case Western has informal articulation agreements with Cuyahoga, Lakeland, and Lorain Community Colleges.

Catholic University

Robert Talbot
Dean of Admissions
Washington, D.C., 20064
(202) 635-5305

Transfer Applicants: 300
Admitted: 150

Articulation Agreements: None

On-Campus Housing: Not Guaranteed
Room & Board: $5000

Tuition: $10,145

Minimum Requirements: 3.0 GPA

Residency: Last 30 credit hours

Mid-Year: Yes

Deadlines: May 1 (Fall)

Colby College

Parker Beverage
Dean of Admissions
Waterville, ME 04901
(800) 343-2052

Transfer Coordinator: Thomas W. Kopp

Transfer Applicants: Fall: 120, Spring: 50
Admitted: Fall: 6–12, Spring: 4–6

Articulation Agreements: None

On-Campus Housing: Yes
Room & Board: $4500

Tuition: $12,000

Minimum Requirements: 3.0 GPA

Residency: 60 sem. credits

Mid-Year: Yes

Deadlines: March 15 (Fall)
Dec. 1 (Spring)

Additional Comments:
Interviews are granted but not required.

Colgate University

Thomas Anthony
Dean of Admissions
Hamilton, NY 13346
(315) 824-1000

Transfer Coordinator: Paul White

Transfer Applicants: 300
Admitted: 30

Articulation Agreements: None

On-Campus Housing: Guaranteed
Room & Board: $4200

Tuition: $12,240

Minimum Requirements: 3.0 GPA

Residency: 4 sems.

Mid-Year: Yes, but usually not freshmen

Deadlines: March 15 (Fall)
Nov. 15 (Spring)

Additional Comments:
Colgate accepts 30% of its freshmen applicants and only 10% of its transfers. The competition is steep. The college transcript is by far the most important aspect of the application, but a student's extracurricular activities are also carefully considered. Colgate provides orientation programs, solely for transfers, for both the fall and spring semesters.

College of William & Mary

G. Gary Ripple
Dean of Admissions
Williamsburg, VA 23185
(804) 253-4223

Transfer Applicants: 900–1100
Admitted: 100–200

Articulation Agreements: (see below)

On-Campus Housing: Not Guaranteed
Room & Board: $3400

Tuition: $2966 in state
$7812 out of state

Minimum Requirements: None (see below)

Residency: 4 sems.

Mid-Year: Yes

Deadlines: Feb. 1 for Part 1 & March 2 for Part 2 (Fall)
Oct. 15 for Part 1 & Nov. 15 for Part 2 (Spring)

Additional Comments:
There are no minimum requirements for transfer admission; however, the average GPA of admitted applicants is 3.5. All applicants must file a two-part application and provide a high school transcript. Transfer students are not required to take the SAT. William & Mary has articulation agreements with Richard Bland College in Petersburg, VA.

College of Wooster

W. A. Hayden Schilling
Dean of Admissions
Wooster, OH 44691
(800) 877-9905

Transfer Coordinator: Byron Morris

Transfer Applicants: 75
Admitted: 50

Articulation Agreements: None

On-Campus Housing: Guaranteed
Room & Board: $3110

Tuition: $14,500 (comprehensive fee)

Minimum Requirements: 2.5 GPA

Residency: 4 sems.

Mid-Year: Yes

Deadlines: June 1 (Fall)
Dec. 1 (Spring)

Columbia University

James T. McMenamin
Director of Admissions
New York, NY 10027
(212) 280-2521

Transfer Coordinator: James F. Minter

Transfer Applicants: Fall: 500–600, Spring: 100–120
Admitted: Fall: 30–40, Spring: 15–20

Articulation Agreements: None

On-Campus Housing: Not Guaranteed
Room & Board: $5400

Tuition: $13,260

Minimum Requirements: 3.0 GPA

Residency: 4 sems.

Mid-Year: Yes

Deadlines: April 1 (Fall)
Oct. 15 (Spring)

Additional Comments:
Columbia students must complete 64 of 124 credits at the college for a bachelor's degree.

Connecticut College

Claire Matthews
Dean of Admissions
New London, CT 06320
(203) 447-7511

Transfer Applicants: 150–200
Admitted: 20–30

Articulation Agreements: None

On-Campus Housing: Guaranteed
Room & Board: $4400

Tuition: $12,900

Minimum Requirements: 3.0 GPA

Residency: 4 sems.

Mid-Year: No

Deadlines: April 1 (Fall)

Cornell University

Nancy Hargrave Meislahan
Director of Admissions
Ithaca, NY 14850
(607) 255-3857

Transfer Coordinator: Deborah Schmidt

Transfer Applicants: 2500
Accepted: 600

Articulation Agreements: (see below)

On-Campus Housing: Not Guaranteed

Room & Board: $4320

Tuition: $4882 in state
$13,100 out of state

Minimum Requirements: 3.0 GPA

Residency: Hotel Administration requires 5 sems. All the rest 4 sems.

Mid-Year: For all colleges except Engineering and the five-year Architecture degree program

Deadlines: March 1 (Fall)
Oct. 15 (Spring)

Additional Comments:
Cornell University's Colleges of Human Ecology, Agriculture, and Life Sciences have articulation agreements with several SUNY two-year colleges.

C. W. Post Center of Long Island University

Stephen Nisenson
Director of Admissions
Greenvale, NY 11548
(516) 299-2413

Transfer Coordinator: Karen McCure

Transfer Applicants: 1246
Admitted: 1013

Articulation Agreements: With Suffolk & Nassau
Community Colleges

On-Campus Housing: Guaranteed
Room & Board: $4200

Tuition: $7480

Minimum Requirements: 2.0 GPA

Residency: 32 credit hours

Mid-Year: Yes

Deadlines: Rolling Admissions

Drew University

William Conley
Admissions Director
Madison, NJ 07940
(201) 377-3000

Transfer Applicants: 120
Admitted: 60

Articulation Agreements: None

On-Campus Housing: Guaranteed
Room & Board: $3400

Tuition: $12,192

Minimum Requirements: 3.0 GPA
approx. 500 SAT

Residency Requirement: 4 sems.

Mid-Year: Yes

Deadlines: July 1 (Fall)
Dec. 1 (Spring)

Additional Comments:
Drew University also requires a minimum 1000 combined SAT score for transfer applicants.

Duke University

Richard Steele
Director of Admissions
Durham, NC 27706
(919) 684-3214

Transfer Applicants: 500
Admitted: 10–50

Articulation Agreements: None

On-Campus Housing: Guaranteed
Room & Board: $4300

Tuition: $12,800

Minimum Requirements: 3.7 GPA

Residency: 16 course credits

Mid-Year: On a space-available basis

Deadlines: 2-part deadline
March 1 & April 1 (Fall)
Sep. 15 & Oct. 15 (Spring)

Evergreen State College

Christine Kerlin
Admissions Director
Olympia, WA 98505
(206) 866-6000

Transfer Applicants: 890

Admitted: 623

Articulation Agreements: Yes

On-Campus Housing: Not Guaranteed
Room & Board: $1400 (room only)

Tuition: $1317 in state
$4581 out of state

Minimum Requirements: 2.0 GPA

Residency: 45 quarter hours

Mid-Year: Yes

Deadlines: March 1 (Fall)
Check with school for winter and spring
deadlines

Fordham University

Richard Avitabile
Admissions Director
Bronx, NY 10458
(212) 579-2133

Transfer Coordinator: Michael Crowley

Transfer Applicants: 688
Admitted: 419

Articulation Agreements: None

On-Campus Housing: Not Guaranteed (see below)
Room & Board: $4900

Tuition: $9280

Minimum Requirements: 3.0 GPA

Residency: 4 sems.

Mid-Year: Yes

Deadlines: July 1 (Fall)
Dec. 1 (Spring)

Additional Comments:
Fordham University considers high school records, SATs, and ACTs for transfer admission, but its greatest focus is placed on the student's college transcript. Even though on-campus housing is not guaranteed, it is available through a lottery. Once in the housing system, transfers are guaranteed housing for the rest of their time at Fordham. There is no visiting students program.

Franklin and Marshall College

Peter Van Buskirk
Director of Admissions
Lancaster, PA 17604-3003
(717) 291-3951

Transfer Applicants: 120
Admitted: 60

Articulation Agreements: None

On-Campus Housing: Not Guaranteed
Room & Board: $4000

Tuition: $13,690

Minimum Requirements: 3.0 GPA

Residency: 4 sems. (16 courses)

Mid-Year: Yes

Deadlines: May 15 (Fall)
Dec. 1 (Spring)

Additional Comments:
Franklin and Marshall carefully reviews transfer candidates' high school records and SAT scores. It also strongly considers a student's extracurricular accomplishments. Offers of admission are determined by both space available in the academic department of the student's intended major and the depth of preparation which the student has demonstrated. From time to time, the college may restrict transfers from entering a specific academic area. Financial aid is available only to students entering in the fall.

Georgetown University

Charles A. Deacon
Dean of Admissions
Washington, D.C. 20057
(202) 687-3600

Transfer Coordinator: Andrea Sears

Transfer Applicants: 1246
Admitted: 260

Articulation Agreements: None

On-Campus Housing: 2 years guaranteed for transfers with sophomore standing. 1 year for transfers with junior standing

Room & Board: $5460

Tuition: $13,250

Minimum Requirements: 3.0 GPA

Residency: 4 sems. (60 sem. hours)

Mid-Year: No

Deadlines: March 1

George Washington University

George Stoner
Dean of Admissions
Washington, D.C. 20052
(202) 994-6040

Transfer Applicants: 1276
Admitted: 1016

Articulation Agreements: None

On-Campus Housing: Not Guaranteed
Room & Board: $5600

Tuition: $11,500

Minimum Requirements: (see below)

Residency: (see below)

Mid-Year: Yes

Deadlines: June 1 (Fall)
Nov. 1 (Spring)

Additional Comments:
Minimum admissions requirements at George Washington University vary according to school. The School of Engineering requires a 2.75 GPA; the School of International Affairs a 3.0 GPA. All other schools require a 2.5 GPA. The residency requirement varies as well. The School of Arts & Sciences requires 45 semester hours to be completed in residence, and all others require 30 semester hours.

Gettysburg College

Delwin Gustafson
Dean of Admissions
Gettysburg, PA 17325
(717) 337-6100
(800) 431-0803

Transfer Coordinator: Delwin Gustafson

Transfer Applicants: 150
Admitted: 45–50

Articulation Agreements: Yes

On-Campus Housing: Guaranteed
Room & Board: $3040

Tuition: $13,625

Minimum Requirements: 2.7 GPA

Residency: 2 sems.

Mid-Year: Yes

Deadlines: Dec. 1 (Fall)
              Feb. 15 (Spring)

Additional Comments:
Gettysburg examines transfer candidates' secondary school record and SAT scores. It will not consider students with GPAs lower than 2.0. Transfer students are accepted for all classes.

Gustavus Adolphus College

Mark Anderson
Admissions Director
Saint Peter, MN 56082
(507) 931-7676

Transfer Applicants: 110–115
Admitted: 60

Articulation Agreements: None

On-Campus Housing: Guaranteed for students admitted
                       prior to April 1
Room & Board: $2700

Tuition: $9850

Minimum Requirements: 2.75 GPA

Residency: 4 sems.

Mid-Year: On a space-available basis

Deadlines: Suggested deadline is April 1

Additional Comments:
Gustavus Adolphus looks for academic progress in its transfer applicants.

Hamilton College

Douglas Thompson
Dean of Admissions
Clinton, NY 13323
(315) 859-4421

Transfer Coordinator: Douglas Thompson

Transfer Applicants: 110
Admitted: 15–20

Articulation Agreements: None

On-Campus Housing: Guaranteed
Room & Board: $4000

Tuition: $12,750

Minimum Requirements: 3.0 GPA

Residency: 4 sems.

Mid-Year: Very few

Deadlines: March 15 (Fall)
           Dec. 1 (Spring)

Harvard University

Marlyn McGrath Louis
Director of Admissions
Cambridge, MA 02138
(617) 495-5309

Transfer Coordinator: Kit Phelps

Transfer Applicants: 1000
Admitted: 120

Articulation Agreements: None

On-Campus Housing: Guaranteed
Room & Board: $4500

Tuition: $12,310

Minimum Requirements: None

Residency: 4 sems.

Mid-Year: Yes

Deadlines: April 15 (Fall)
          Feb. 15 (Spring)

Additional Comments:
Harvard University has no minimum requirements for admission.

Harvey Mudd College

Duncan C. Murdoch
Dean of Admissions
301 E. Twelfth St.
Claremont, CA 91711-5990
(714) 621-8011

Transfer Applicants: 30–50
Admitted: 10–15

Articulation Agreements: None

On-Campus Housing: Not guaranteed but 95% of students live on campus
Room & Board: $5290

Tuition: $12,690

Minimum Requirements: 2.5 GPA

Residency: 4 sems.

Mid-Year: Yes

Deadlines: May 1

Additional Comments:
The SAT and ACT are optional, but the Math II and English Achievement tests are strongly recommended for admission. Students may not transfer to Harvey Mudd College as seniors.

Haverford College

Delsie Phillips
Director of Admissions
Haverford, PA 19041
(215) 896-1350

Transfer Applicants: 125–140
Admitted: 4–8

Articulation Agreements: None

On-Campus Housing: Guaranteed
Room & Board: $4400

Tuition: $12,525

Minimum Requirements: 3.0 GPA

Residency: 4 sems.

Mid-Year: No

Deadlines: March 31

Hofstra University

Joan Issac
Admissions Director
Hempstead, NY 11550
(516) 560-6700

Transfer Applicants: 2300
Admitted: 1640

Articulation Agreements: Yes

On-Campus Housing: Guaranteed
Room & Board: $4300

Tuition: $7730

Minimum Requirements: 2.5 GPA

Residency: 2 sems.

Mid-Year: Yes

Deadlines: June 1 (Fall)
          Jan. 1 (Spring)

Kalamazoo College

David Borus
Director of Admissions
Kalamazoo, MI 49007
(616) 383-8408

Transfer Coordinator: Anne Okon

Transfer Applicants: 55
Admitted: 40

Articulation Agreements: None

On-Campus Housing: Guaranteed for the first year
Room & Board: $3516

Tuition: $10,487

Minimum Requirements: 2.8 GPA

Residency: 3 terms (1 year)

Mid-Year: On a space-available basis

Deadlines: June 1 (Fall)
Oct. 1 (Spring)

Additional Comments:
Kalamazoo requires that all candidates have SAT scores of
500M/500V or a composite ACT score of 23. The admissions
office said that they accept mid-year applicants "reluctantly."

Kenyon College

John Anderson
Dean of Admissions
Gambier, OH 43022-9623
(800) 282-2459 (in state)
(800) 848-2468 (out of state)

Transfer Applicants: 80–100
Admitted: 10–20

Articulation Agreements: None

On-Campus Housing: Guaranteed
Room & Board: $3050

Tuition: $11,555

Minimum Requirements: 3.0 GPA

Residency: 4 sems.

Mid-Year: On a space-available basis

Deadlines: May 1 (Fall)
Nov. 15 (Spring)

Lafayette College

Bradley Quin
Director of Admissions
Easton, PA 18042
(215) 250-5100

Transfer Coordinator: Jennifer Seller

Transfer Applicants: Fall: 100–150, Spring: 80–100
Admitted: Fall: 10–20, Spring: 5–10

Articulation Agreements: None

On-Campus Housing: Guaranteed
Room & Board: $4300

Tuition: $12,025

Minimum Requirements: 3.0 GPA

Residency: ½ total number of credits

Mid-Year: Yes

Deadlines: Dec. 15 (Spring)
June 1 (Fall)

Additional Comments:
Lafayette looks closely at the program of study, college or
university of transfer, and the high school record. The SAT or
ACT is required but not necessarily for nontraditional students.
Students may only transfer to Lafayette up to half the total
number of credits required for their degree program.

Lawrence University

Steven Syverson
Dean of Admissions
Appleton, WI 54912
(414) 735-6500
(800) 227-0982 (out of state)

Transfer Applicants: 81
Admitted: 53

Articulation Agreements: None

On-Campus Housing: Guaranteed

Room & Board: $2300

Tuition: $10,770

Minimum Requirements: 3.0 GPA

Residency: 6 trimesters

Mid-Year: Yes

Deadlines: May 15

Middlebury College

Fred F. Neuberger
Dean of Admissions
Middlebury, VT 05753
(802) 388-3711

Transfer Applicants: 275
Admitted: 20

Articulation Agreements: (see below)

On-Campus Housing: Guaranteed
Room & Board: n/a

Tuition: $19,000 (comprehensive fee)

Minimum Requirements: 3.0 GPA

Residency: 2 years

Mid-Year: Yes

Deadlines: March 1

Additional Comments:
Middlebury has articulation agreements with Montgomery, LaGuardia, Bronx, and Miami-Dade Community Colleges.

Mount Holyoke College

Susan Staggers
Dean of Admissions and Financial Aid
South Hadley, MA 01075-1488
(413) 538-2023

Transfer Coordinator: Majorie Southworth-Purdy

Transfer Applicants: 176
Admitted: 71

Articulation Agreements: None

On-Campus Housing: Guaranteed
Room & Board: $4300

Tuition: $12,840

Minimum Requirements: 3.0 GPA

Residency: 64 credit hours

Mid-Year: Yes

Deadlines: Feb. 15 (Fall)
Dec. 1 (Spring)

Additional Comments:
Mount Holyoke does not offer financial aid for mid-year transfers.

New College
University of South Florida

Robert Thorton
Director of Admissions
Sarasota, FL 34243-2197
(813) 355-2963
(813) 355-7671

Transfer Applicants: n/a
Admitted: 75

Articulation Agreements: None

On-Campus Housing: Not guaranteed
Room & Board: $3050

Tuition: $1400 in state
$4400 out of state

Minimum Requirements: None

Residency: 4 sems. plus 2 January Independent Study terms

Mid-Year: Yes

Deadlines: July 1 (Fall)
Dec. 15 (Spring)

Additional Comments:
New College is not grade and score sensitive. They are interested in highly motivated, intelligent, and capable people. Transfer students are not tracked separately from other applicants.

Northwestern University

Carol Lunkenheimer
Director of Admissions
Evanston, IL 60043
(312) 491-7271

Transfer Coordinator: Joan Miller

Transfer Applicants: 575
Admitted: 133

Articulation Agreements: None

On-Campus Housing: Not guaranteed
Room & Board: $4380

Tuition: $12,270

Minimum Requirements: 3.0 GPA

Residency: 6 quarters

Mid-Year: Yes

Deadlines: June 1 (Fall)
Nov. 1 (Winter)
Feb. 1 (Spring)
May 1 (Summer)

Additional Comments:
Northwestern's Medill School of Journalism and Department of Radio-Television-Film do not accept transfer students. Candidates for the Theatre Department are encouraged to apply for the fall quarter only. Transfer credit is given for Advanced Placement courses taken in high school. Interviews are strongly recommended.

Oklahoma State University

Robin Lacey
Admissions Director
Stillwater, OK 74078
(405) 744-6876

Transfer Applicants: 2328
Admitted: 2025

Articulation Agreements: Yes

On-Campus Housing: Guaranteed
Room & Board: $2700

Tuition: $1100 in state
$4000 out of state

Minimum Requirements: (see below)

Residency: ½ of the upper division requirements & the last 18–30 hours (varies by college)

Mid-Year: Yes

Deadlines: Rolling Admissions

Additional Comments:
Applicants to the Oklahoma State University with fewer than 24 hours of credit must have a 1.4 GPA and meet freshman admissions standards. Applicants with 24–36 hours need a 1.6 GPA; applicants with 37–72 hours a 1.8 GPA; and applicants with 73 or more credit hours a 2.0 GPA.

Pomona College

Bruce J. Poch
Dean of Admissions
Claremont, CA 91711
(714) 621-8134

Transfer Applicants: Numbers vary, roughly 200+
Admitted: 10 to 15%

Articulation Agreements: None

On-Campus Housing: Guaranteed
Room & Board: $5200

Tuition: $12,620

Minimum Requirements: None

Residency: 16 sem. credits

Mid-Year: No

Deadlines: April 1

Additional Comments:
There are no minimum requirements at Pomona and criteria for admission vary dramatically because of the disparity in the applicant pool. However, the transfer pool is extremely competitive because very few students leave. The Admissions Committee places considerable weight on the nature and quality of the previous college record.

Princeton University

Anthony Cummings
Dean of Admissions
Princeton, NJ 08544
(609) 452-3060

Transfer Applicants: 400
Admitted: 20

Articulation Agreements: None

On-Campus Housing: Yes
Room & Board: $4817

Tuition: $14,390

Minimum Requirements: None, but a 3.5 GPA is recommended

Residency: 4 sems.

Mid-Year: No

Deadlines: March 1

Reed College

Robert Mansueto
Dean of Admissions
Portland, OR 97202
(503) 777-7511
(800) 547-4750

Transfer Applicants: 204
Admitted: 122

Articulation Agreements: None

On-Campus Housing: Not guaranteed
Room & Board: $3870

Tuition: $11,240

Minimum Requirements: None

Residency: 4 sems.

Mid-Year: Yes

Deadlines: April 1 (Fall)
              Dec. 1 (Spring)

Rensselaer Polytechnic Institute

Conrad Sharrow
Dean of Admissions
Troy, NY 12180-3590
(518) 266-6216

Transfer Applicants: 500
Admitted: 300

Articulation Agreements: With 30 junior colleges
                            nationwide

On-Campus Housing: Guaranteed
Room & Board: $3850

Tuition: $12,250

Minimum Requirements: 3.0 GPA

Residency: 4 sems.

Mid-Year: Yes

Deadlines: April 1 (Fall)
              Nov. 1 (Spring)

Additional Comments:
Transfer students are accepted at Rensselaer for the freshman
and sophomore classes.

Rhodes College

David Wottle
Dean of Admissions
Memphis, TN 38112
(901) 726-3700

Transfer Applicants: 70
Admitted: 25

Articulation Agreements: None

On-Campus Housing: Not guaranteed
Room & Board: $3824

Tuition: $10,660

Minimum Requirements: 2.5 GPA

Residency: 4 sems.

Mid-Year: Yes

Deadlines: Feb. 1 (Fall)
　　　　　　Nov. 15 (Spring)

Additional Comments:
In addition to a 2.5 GPA, applicants to Rhodes are expected to
have a 1000 combined SAT score. Students must complete 56
credits at the college.

Skidmore College

Kent Jones
Admissions Director
Saratoga Springs, NY 12866
(518) 587-7569

Transfer Coordinator: Larry Lichtenstein

Transfer Applicants: 160
Admitted: 50

Articulation Agreements: None

On-Campus Housing: Not guaranteed
Room & Board: $4300

Tuition: $12,255

Minimum Requirements: (see below)

Residency: 4 sems.

Mid-Year: On a space-available basis

Deadlines: April 1 (Fall)
Nov. 15 (Spring)

Additional Comments:
Skidmore does not have minimum requirements, but most admitted transfers have a 3.0 GPA or better. The median SAT scores are much the same as those for freshmen: 550 verbal and 600 math, composite ACT score of 26.

Smith College

Lorna Blake
Admissions Director
Northhampton, MA 01063
(413) 585-2500

Transfer Coordinator: Sidonia Dalby

Transfer Applicants: 259
Admitted: 142

Articulation Agreements: None

On-Campus Housing: Guaranteed
Room & Board: $5170

Tuition: $12,120

Minimum Requirements: (see below)

Residency: 4 sems.

Mid-Year: Yes

Deadlines: Feb. 15 (Fall)
Nov. 15 (Spring)

Additional Comments:
Smith suggests a minimum GPA of 3.0, but weighs heavily the types of college courses taken and the reasons for transferring. SAT and high school transcript are also required.

Southern Illinois University Carbondale

Jerre Pfaff
Director of Admissions
Carbondale, IL 62901
(618) 453-4381

Transfer Applicants: Fall: 5808, Spring: 2888, Summer: 1109
Admitted: Fall: 4167, Spring: 1513, Summer: 940

Articulation Agreements: Yes

On-Campus Housing: Not guaranteed
Room & Board: $2600

Tuition: $1560 in state
$4680 out of state

Minimum Requirements: 2.0 GPA (see below)

Residency: 60 sem. hours

Mid-Year: Yes

Deadlines: Rolling Admissions

Additional Comments:
Admission requirements to the Southern University of Illinois at Carbondale vary according to department. The Business School requires a 2.5 GPA, Engineering 2.4, and Communications 2.25.

Stanford University

Jean Fetter
Dean of Admissions
Stanford, CA 94305
(415) 497-2091

Transfer Applicants: 1211
Admitted: 97

Articulation Agreements: None

On-Campus Housing: Guaranteed
Room & Board: $5257

Tuition: $13,569

Minimum Requirements: (see below)

Residency: 90 quarter units

Mid-Year: No

Deadlines: March 15

Additional Comments:
Stanford looks for students with "a strong liberal arts background, evidence of co-curricular activity, and well-articulated reasons for wanting to transfer." Interviews are not provided. There is no visiting students program. Stanford does have an Affirmative Action program. The SAT or ACT is required.

State University of New York Binghamton

Geoffery Gould
Admissions Director
Binghamton, NY 13901
(607) 777-2171

Transfer Applicants: 3500–4000
Admitted: 300–700 enrolled

Articulation Agreements: Yes

On-Campus Housing: (see below)
Room & Board: $3388

Tuition: $1350 in state
$3950 out of state

Minimum Requirements: (see below)

Residency: 2 sems.

Mid-Year: On a space-available basis

Deadlines: Rolling Admissions

Additional Comments:
Transfers to SUNY Binghamton are housed in university-run apartments close to, but not on, campus. Admissions standards vary by academic department and are based on "supply and demand." The SAT or ACT is not required for transfer students.

State University of New York
Geneseo

Janet Graeter
Dean of Admissions
Geneseo, NY 14454
(716) 245-5571

Transfer Coordinator: Scott Hookes

Transfer Applicants: 1700
Admitted: 316

Articulation Agreements: Yes

On-Campus Housing: Guaranteed
Room & Board: $3000

Tuition: $1350 in state
$3950 out of state

Minimum Requirements: 3.0 GPA

Residency: 2 sems. (30 credit hours)

Mid-Year: On a space-available basis

Deadlines: Feb. 15 (Fall)
Nov. 15 (Spring)

Additional Comments:
In order to be a viable candidate for transfer admission at
SUNY Geneseo, applicants must have a 3.0 GPA. Most students, however, have a GPA of 3.3 or higher.

State University of New York
New Paltz

Robert Seamen
Admissions Director
New Paltz, NY 12516
(914) 257-2414

Transfer Coordinator: Valerie Eldridge

Transfer Applicants: 2852
Admitted: 1646

Articulation Agreements: (see below)

On-Campus Housing: Guaranteed
Room & Board: $3000

Tuition: $1350 in state
$3950 out of state

Minimum Requirements: (see below)

Residency: 30 credit hours

Mid-Year: Yes

Deadlines: May 15 (Fall)
Nov. 15 (Spring)

Additional Comments:
Graduates of Ulster, Rockland, Dutchess, Hudson Valley, Sullivan, Orange, and Borough of Manhattan Colleges with an AA or AS degree are guaranteed admission to SUNY New Paltz but not necessarily to the program of their choice. Applicants to the programs of Business, Communication, and Elementary Education need a 2.5 GPA. All others need a 2.3.

State University of New York
Oswego

Joseph Grant
Admissions Director
Oswego, NY 13126
(315) 341-2250

Transfer Applicants: 3103
Admitted: 1229

Articulation Agreements: Yes

On-Campus Housing: Guaranteed
Room & Board: $3100

Tuition: $1350 in state
$3950 out of state

Minimum Requirements: 2.5 GPA

Residency: 2 sems.

Mid-Year: Yes

Deadlines: Rolling Admissions

Additional Comments:
SUNY Oswego gives preference to applications received by Jan. 13 for the fall term.

Trinity College

Donald Dietrich
Admissions Director
Hartford, CT 06106
(203) 527-3151

Transfer Coordinator: Larry Dow

Transfer Applicants: 220
Admitted: 40

Articulation Agreements: None

On-Campus Housing: Not guaranteed
Room & Board: $4000

Tuition: $12,380

Minimum Requirements: 3.0 GPA

Residency: 4 sems. (16 courses)

Mid-Year: Yes

Deadlines: March 15 (Fall)
             Nov. 15 (Spring)

Trinity University

Alberta Meyer
Admissions Director
San Antonio, TX 78284
(512) 736-7207

Transfer Applicants: 150

Admitted: 75

Articulation Agreements: None

On-Campus Housing: Guaranteed
Room & Board: $3800

Tuition: $8880

Minimum Requirements: 3.0 GPA

Residency: 4 sems. (60 credit hours)

Mid-Year: Yes

Deadlines: April 15

Union College

Kenneth Nourse
Dean of Admissions
Schenectady, NY 12308
(518) 370-6112

Transfer Applicants: 130
Admitted: 60

Articulation Agreements: (see below)

On-Campus Housing: Not guaranteed
Room & Board: $4500

Tuition: $12,175

Minimum Requirements: 3.0 GPA

Residency: 6 terms

Mid-Year: On a space-available basis

Deadlines: June 15 (Fall)
Nov. 1 (Winter)
Feb. 1 (Spring)

Additional Comments:
Students with a 3.0 GPA in Engineering Science at the colleges listed above are guaranteed junior standing at Union. Acceptance for all transfers is on a rolling basis. Courses in business or engineering technologies do not transfer. Union's visiting students program has the same requirements as for transferring. The School of Engineering has articulation agreements with Broome, Dutchess County, Fulton-Montgomery, Hudson Valley, and Mohawk Valley Community Colleges.

University of Arizona

Jerome Lucido
Admissions Director
Tucson, AZ 85721
(602) 621-3237

Transfer Applicants: 4900
Admitted: 2900

Articulation Agreements: (see below)

On-Campus Housing: Not guaranteed
Room & Board: $3200

Tuition: $0 in state
$4200 out of state

Minimum Requirements: 2.5 GPA

Residency: 30 credit hours

Mid-Year: Yes

Deadlines: Aug. 1 (Fall)
Dec. 1 (Spring)
May 1 (Summer)

Additional Comments:
The University of Arizona has articulation agreements with every two-year college in the state. Each college within the university has its own entrance requirements.

University of California
Berkeley

Robert Bailey
Director of Admissions
Berkeley, CA 94720
(415) 642-6667

Transfer Applicants: 5000
Admitted: 2000+

Articulation Agreements: (see below)

On-Campus Housing: Not guaranteed
Room & Board: $5000

Tuition: $0 in state
$6000 out of state

Minimum Requirements: (see below)

Residency: Last 24 sem. hours

Mid-Year: In most majors

Deadlines: Nov. (Fall)
July (Spring)

Additional Comments:
The University of California at Berkeley has articulation agreements with all ninety California community colleges. Agreements are by department and are on a course-for-course equivalency system. Berkeley only accepts transfers with 56 transferable semester units (junior standing). The minimum requirements for admission vary by department but a 2.0 GPA is needed if the student was eligible as a high school applicant, a 2.4 if not, and a 2.8 if the applicant is from out of state.

University of California
San Diego

Ronald Bowker
Admissions Director
Lajolla, CA 92093
(213) 534-3160

Transfer Applicants: 3400
Admitted: 1400

Articulation Agreements: Yes

On-Campus Housing: Guaranteed for 1 year
Room & Board: $5421

Tuition: $0 in state
$6600 out of state

Minimum Requirements: 2.4 GPA (see below)

Residency: 36 credit hours

Mid-Year: On a space-available basis

Deadlines: Nov. 30 (Fall)
          July 31 (Winter)
          Oct. 31 (Spring)
          (see below)

Additional Comments:
Transfer applicants to U.C. San Diego with fewer than 56 semester hours (or 84 quarter hours) of transferable credit must meet the requirements for freshman admission. The minimum GPA for out-of-state applicants is 2.8. The dates listed above for application are "priority deadlines," and represent the final date in a priority period (the period lasts the entire month). The university does accept applications after these deadlines.

University of California
Santa Barbara

William Villa
Admissions Director
Santa Barbara, CA 93106
(805) 961-3426

Transfer Applicants: 375
Admitted: 114

Articulation Agreements: None

On-Campus Housing: Not guaranteed
Room & Board: $5520

Tuition: $0 in state
          $6500 out of state

Minimum Requirements: 2.75 GPA

Residency: 4 sems. (56 sem. hours)

Mid-Year: Yes

Deadlines: March 1 (Fall)

Additional Comments:
Applicants to U.C. Santa Barbara must have completed 30 transferable semester units at their previous institution. Approximately twenty students are admitted each spring term.

University of California
Santa Cruz

Joseph Allen
Admissions Director
Santa Cruz, CA 95064
(408) 429-4008

Transfer Coordinator: Donna Mekis

Transfer Applicants: 1428 junior college applicants
Admitted: 740

Articulation Agreements: With 35 California community
colleges (see below)

On-Campus Housing: Not guaranteed
Room & Board: $4800

Tuition: $0 in state
$4800 out of state

Minimum Requirements: (see below)

Residency: 56 credit hours

Mid-Year: On a space-available basis

Deadlines: Nov. 1–30 (Fall)
July 1–31 (Winter)
Oct. 1–31 (Spring)

Additional Comments:
The University of Santa Cruz receives transfer applications
from students across the country but in the past few years was
only able to admit graduates of California community colleges.
First priority is always given to minority students, and when
space is available, to applicants from other U.C. campuses. The
university does not grant interviews for transfer applicants but
provides counseling for community college students. Requirements differ for each of the undergraduate departments.

University of Chicago

Theodore O'Neil
Admissions Director
Chicago, IL 60637
(312) 702-8650

Transfer Applicants: 325
Admitted: 75–100

Articulation Agreements: None

On-Campus Housing: Yes
Room & Board: $5200

Tuition: $13,815

Minimum Requirements: 3.4 GPA

Residency: 8 quarters

Mid-Year: Rarely

Deadlines: April 1 for a May 1 notification
May 1 for a June 1 notification
On a space-available basis until July 1

University of Delaware

N. Bruce Walker
Admissions Director
Newark, DE 19716
(302) 451-8123

Transfer Applicants: 1999
Admitted: 1034

Articulation Agreements: (see below)

On-Campus Housing: Not guaranteed
Room & Board: $2740

Tuition: $2560 in state
$6300 out of state

Minimum Requirements: (see below)

Residency: First 90 or last 30 credit hours

Mid-Year: Yes

Deadlines: March 1 (Fall)
Nov. 15 (Spring)

Additional Comments:
Delaware resident applicants to the University of Delaware must have at least a 2.0 GPA; out-of-state applicants need a 2.5 GPA. Some departments (including Engineering, Business Administration, Economics, Elementary Teacher Education, and Computer Science) require much higher grade point averages.

University of Florida

S. William Kolb
Admissions Director
Gainesville, FL 32611
(904) 392-1365

Transfer Applicants: 7500
Admitted: 2500

Articulation Agreements: With all Florida public junior
colleges (see below)

On-Campus Housing: Not guaranteed
Room & Board: $3200

Tuition: $1150 in state
$3700 out of state

Minimum Requirements: Varies greatly

Residency: 30 sem. hours

Mid-Year: Yes

Deadlines: Check with school for deadlines appropriate to
your needs

Additional Comments:

Transfers must opt to apply either to the lower division or the
upper division schools. A lower division undergraduate transfer
must have been eligible for admission as a freshman, must be
in "good academic standing," and must have a 2.0 GPA. D
grades transfer. An upper division undergraduate transfer must
have passed the College Level Academic Skills Test (CLAST).
Florida public junior college graduates with an AA degree are
guaranteed admission to the upper division (some restrictions
do apply).

University of Georgia

Claire Swann
Admissions Director
Athens, GA 30602
(404) 542-2112

Transfer Applicants: 8000–10,000
Admitted: 6400–8000

Articulation Agreements: Yes, statewide

On-Campus Housing: No
Room & Board: $2600

Tuition: $1579 in state
$4736 out of state

Minimum Requirements: 2.0 GPA

Residency: 3 quarters

Mid-Year: Yes

Deadlines: Aug. 1 (Fall)
Dec. 1 (Winter)
March 1 (Spring)
May 1 (Summer)

University of Idaho

Matthew Telin
Admissions Director
Moscow, ID 83843
(208) 885-6326

Transfer Applicants: 1100
Admitted: 975

Articulation Agreements: Yes

On-Campus Housing: Guaranteed
Room & Board: $2400

Tuition: $0 in state
$2000 out of state

Minimum Requirements: 2.0 GPA (see below)

Residency: 2 sems.

Mid-Year: Yes

Deadlines: July 1

Additional Comments:
The College of Engineering requires a 2.8 GPA for admission.

University of Iowa

Michael Barron
Admissions Director
Iowa City, IA 52242

Transfer Applicants: 2874
Admitted: 1887

Articulation Agreements: Yes

On-Campus Housing: n/a
Room & Board: $2580

Tuition: $1800 in state
$6000 out of state

Minimum Requirements: 2.25 GPA; 24 sem. hours of
transferable credit

Residency: Final 2 sems. (30 sem. hours) or 45 out of last 60
sem. hours

Mid-Year: Yes

Deadlines (for Liberal Arts): May 15 (Fall & Summer)
Nov. 15 (Spring)

University of Michigan

Cliff Sjogren
Director of Admissions
Ann Arbor, MI 48109
(313) 764-7433

Transfer Coordinator: Eleanor M. Hendershot

Transfer Applicants: 4213
Admitted: 2372

Articulation Agreements: With all Michigan junior colleges

On-Campus Housing: Not guaranteed
Room & Board: $3640

Tuition: $3194 in state
$10,614 out of state

Minimum Requirements: 2.5 GPA

Residency: 60 sem. hours. For Engineering, Education, and Natural Resources: 30 sem. hours

Mid-Year: In some units, yes (LSA, Music, Art)
In others, Fall only (Education, Engineering)

Deadlines: Feb. 15 (Spring, Summer, Fall)
Nov. 1 (Winter)

Additional Comments:
The SAT or ACT is required only for Michigan's Education Department. The level of college course work is a significant criterion for transfer admission. Preference is given to Michigan residents.

University of Minnesota

Robert Vicander
Admissions Director
Morris, MN 56267
(612) 589-2116

Transfer Applicants: 180–200
Admitted: 50–70

Articulation Agreements: None

On-Campus Housing: Not guaranteed
Room & Board: $2700

Tuition: $1850 in state
$4626 out of state

Minimum Requirements: 2.5 GPA

Residency: 45 quarter hours

Mid-Year: Yes

Deadlines: April 15 (Fall)
Nov. 15 (Spring)

University of Missouri
Rolla

Robert Louis
Admissions Director
Rolla, MO 65401
(314) 341-4156

Transfer Applicants: 450
Admitted: 400

Articulation Agreements: With 44 midwestern community
colleges

On-Campus Housing: Not guaranteed (see below)
Room & Board: $3200

Tuition: $1800 in state
$5300 out of state

Minimum Requirements: 2.5 GPA (see below)

Residency: 45 of the last 60 credit hours

Mid-Year: Yes

Deadlines: July 1 (Fall)
Dec. 1 (Spring)
May 1 (Summer)

Additional Comments:
Although the University of Missouri at Rolla does not
guarantee housing, the admissions office says that "ample
housing is available both on campus and in the community."
The Electrical Engineering Department requires a 3.0 GPA.

University of Nebraska

John Beacon
Admissions Director
Lincoln, NE 68588
(402) 472-3620

Transfer Applicants: 1400–1700
Admitted: 1200–1300

Articulation Agreements: Yes

On-Campus Housing: Not guaranteed
Room & Board: $2200

Tuition: $1790 in state
$4140 out of state

Minimum Requirements: 2.0 GPA

Residency: 30 of the last 36 credit hours

Mid-Year: Yes

Deadlines: Rolling Admissions (see below)

Additional Comments:
The University of Nebraska at Lincoln has varying requirements for some majors. The College of Architecture requires a 2.6–3.0 GPA, Business Administration and the Teachers College a 2.5. February 1 is the "preferred" deadline for summer session and October 1 for the spring semester.

University of Nevada
Las Vegas

Larry Mason
Admissions Director
Las Vegas, NV 89154
(702) 739-3443

Transfer Coordinator: Carl D. Cook

Transfer Applicants: n/a
Admitted: 2500

Articulation Agreements: Yes

On-Campus Housing: Not guaranteed
Room & Board: $3800

Tuition: $1240 in state
$4240 out of state

Minimum Requirements: 2.0 GPA

Residency: 30 sem. hours

Mid-Year: Yes

Deadlines: Aug. 16 (Fall)
Dec. 15 (Spring)

Additional Comments:
All students applying to the University of Nevada must have
completed 15 transferable credits at their previous institution.

University of North Carolina Chapel Hill

Richard Cashwell
Admissions Director
Chapel Hill, NC 27514
(919) 966-3621

Transfer Coordinator: Jean P. Girtman

Transfer Applicants: 2100
Admitted: 750

Articulation Agreements: None

On-Campus Housing: Not guaranteed
Room & Board: $3055

Tuition: $504 in state
　　　　$4106 out of state

Minimum Requirements: (see below)

Residency: 2 sems. and half of all courses in major

Mid-Year: Very rarely

Deadlines: March 1 (Fall)
　　　　Oct. 15 (Spring)
　　　　(see below)

Additional Comments:
UNC at Chapel Hill has varying admissions requirements for
each major but does not require SAT scores. Arts & Science
majors require a minimum 3.0 GPA for North Carolina
residents and 3.5 GPA for out-of-state applicants. Junior transfers need at least 51 transferable credits.

University of Oregon

James Birch
Director of Admissions
Eugene, OR 97403
(503) 686-4091

Transfer Applicants: 2000
Admitted: 1000+

Articulation Agreements: With all Oregon community
colleges

On-Campus Housing: Not guaranteed
Room & Board: $2600

Tuition: $1679 in state
$4547 out of state

Minimum Requirements: (see below)

Residency: 45 of last 60 quarter hours

Mid-Year: Yes

Deadlines: May 1 (Fall)
March 1 (Spring)

Additional Comments:
The University of Oregon accepts all applicants from Oregon
community colleges with AA degrees. For other Oregon resident
applicants, a minimum of 2.25 GPA is required. Out-of-state
applicants need at least a 2.5 GPA.

University of Pennsylvania

Willis Stetson
Dean of Admissions
Philadelphia, PA 19104
(215) 898-7507

Transfer Coordinator: Elizabeth O'Connel

Transfer Applicants: Fall: 1000, Spring: 300
Admitted: Fall: 400–450, Spring: 100

Articulation Agreements: None

On-Campus Housing: Guaranteed
Room & Board: $3300

Tuition: $11,678

Minimum Requirements: (see below)

Residency: 4 sems.

Mid-Year: Yes

Deadlines: April 1 (Fall)
Oct. 15 (Spring)

Additional Comments:
The University of Pennsylvania does not have a minimum grade point average requirement for admission but strongly recommends a 3.4 GPA. Sophomore applicants to the Wharton School need one year of calculus and one year of economics; junior applicants also need one year of accounting. All applicants to the School of Engineering need one year of calculus and one year of physics.

University of Richmond

Thomas Pollard
Dean of Admissions
Richmond, VA 23173
(804) 289-8640

Transfer Applicants: 300+
Admitted: 40–50

Articulation Agreements: None

On-Campus Housing: Not guaranteed
Room & Board: $2500

Tuition: $9130

Minimum Requirements: 2.0 GPA

Residency: 60 credit hours

Mid-Year: Yes

Deadlines: Feb. 1 (Fall)
Nov. 1 (Spring)

University of South Alabama

J. David Sterns
Admissions Director
Mobile, AL 36688
(205) 460-6141

Transfer Applicants: 1500
Admitted: 900

Articulation Agreements: (see below)

On-Campus Housing: Not guaranteed
Room & Board: $2508

Tuition: $1584 in state
$2184 out of state

Minimum Requirements: 2.0 GPA

Residency: 48 quarter hours

Mid-Year: Yes

Deadlines: Sept. 10 (Fall)
Dec. 10 (Winter)
March 10 (Spring)
June 1 (Summer)

Additional Comments:
Some colleges within the University of South Alabama have articulation agreements with local junior colleges; check with the school to which you are applying. A high school transcript is required if you have fewer than 40 transferable quarter (or 30 semester) hours. Housing availability for transfers is "usually ample," according to the admissions office.

University of Southern California

Director of Admissions
Los Angeles, CA
90089-0911
(213) 743-6741

Transfer Coordinator: Sandi Cazenave

Transfer Applicants: Fall: 4000, Spring: 1500
Admitted: 2000 annually

Articulation Agreements: With all 107 California
community colleges

On-Campus Housing: Not guaranteed (see below)

Room & Board: $4140

Tuition: $12,244

Minimum Requirements: (see below)

Residency: last 48 credit hours (3 sems.)

Mid-Year: Yes

Deadlines: Check with school

Additional Comments:
USC guarantees housing only for first-year students, but according to the admissions office, "all students who meet the housing deadlines are usually housed." The university does not have a set minimum grade point average, but a 2.7 (B−) is generally required. Test scores are not required except for the Departments of Journalism and Architecture, which also require high school transcripts.

University of Tennessee
Chattanooga

Patsy Renolds
Admissions Director
Chattanooga, TN 37403
(615) 755-4662

Transfer Applicants: 874
Admitted: 685

Articulation Agreements: With Chattanooga State
                            community colleges

On-Campus Housing: Not guaranteed
Room & Board: $2000

Tuition: $1222 in state
         $3956 out of state

Minimum Requirements: (see below)

Residency: Last 30 sem. hours

Mid-Year: Yes

Deadlines: Rolling Admissions

Additional Comments:
Applicants to the University of Tennessee at Chattanooga with fewer than 23 semester hours need a 1.0 GPA. Applicants with 24–39 hours need a 1.5. Applicants with 40–55 hours need a 1.8, and those with more than 56 hours need a 2.0 GPA.

University of Texas
Austin

Shirley Binder
Admissions Director
Austin, TX 78712
(512) 471-1711

Transfer Applicants: 10,000
Admitted: 5300

Articulation Agreements: (see below)

On-Campus Housing: Not guaranteed
Room & Board: $3300

Tuition: $480 in state
             $3600 out of state

Minimum Requirements: (see below)

Residency: 24 of last 30 sem. hours

Mid-Year: Yes

Deadlines: March 1 (Fall)
              Oct. 1 (Spring)
              March 1 (Summer)

Additional Comments:
The University of Texas at Austin does not have formal articulation agreements with any junior colleges; however, it does provide general transfer equivalency guides listing JC courses and their U.T. equivalent. Applicants with fewer than 53 transferable semester hours of credit need a 3.0 GPA. Applicants with 54 or more need a 2.5. There are separate admissions requirements for out-of-state applicants.

University of Washington

Admissions Office
Seattle, WA 98195
(206) 543-9686

Transfer Coordinator: Rebecca Evans

Transfer Applicants: 5694
Admitted: 2664

Articulation Agreements: Yes

On-Campus Housing: Guaranteed
Room & Board: $3000

Tuition: $1731 in state
$4800 out of state

Minimum Requirements: (see below)

Residency: 45 credits

Mid-Year: Yes

Deadlines: March 15 (Summer/Fall)
Nov. 1 (Winter)
Feb. 1 (Spring)

Additional Comments:
Transfer applicants at the University of Washington are ranked according to an admissions index. This AI is based on a combination of test scores and grades and varies from quarter to quarter. Applicants must complete at least 45 quarter hours of transferable credit at their previous institution. High school grades are also considered if fewer than 45 credits have been completed. Out-of-state applicants are expected to meet admission standards "substantially higher" than those required for Washington residents.

University of Wisconsin
Madison

David Vinson
Admissions Director
Madison, WI 53706
(608) 262-3961

Transfer Applicants: 3774
Admitted: 1950

Articulation Agreements: With the University of Wisconsin
Centers

On-Campus Housing: Not guaranteed
Room & Board: $3100

Tuition: $1857 in state
$5639 out of state

Minimum Requirements: 2.5 GPA and 24 credits

Residency: 2 sems.

Mid-Year: Yes

Deadlines: March 1 (Fall)
Nov. 15 (Spring)
March 1 (Summer)

Vassar College

James Kaeting
Admissions Director
Poughkeepsie, NY 12601
(914) 452-7000

Transfer Coordinator: Richard N. George, Jr.

Transfer Applicants: Fall: 250, Spring: 100
Admitted: Fall: 40–50, Spring: 15–25

Articulation Agreements: (see below)

On-Campus Housing: Guaranteed
Room & Board: $4250

Tuition: $12,300

Minimum Requirements: 3.0 GPA

Residency: 4 sems. (17 courses)

Mid-Year: Yes

Deadlines: March 1 (Fall)
Nov. 15 (Spring)

Additional Comments:
Vassar is one of five private colleges to receive funds as part of
a nationwide effort to increase the number of students who
transfer from two-year to four-year schools. Vassar has articulation agreements with LaGuardia, Borough of Manhattan,
Dutchess, Ulster, Sullivan, and Rockland Community Colleges.

Villanova University

Rev. Harry Erdlen
Dean of Admissions
Villanova, PA 19085-1672
(215) 645-4000

Transfer Applicants: 320
Admitted: 100

Articulation Agreements: None

On-Campus Housing: Not guaranteed (see below)
Room & Board: $4500

Tuition: $9000

Minimum Requirements: 2.5 GPA for Engineering and Science, 3.0 GPA for Arts

Residency: 2 sems.

Mid-Year: On a very limited basis

Deadlines: April 15 (Fall)
Nov. 15 (Spring)

Additional Comments:
On-campus housing at Villanova is not available for transfer students. However, the Office for Residence Life does assist students in finding off-campus accommodations. Although formal articulation agreements do not exist, community college transfer students are given preference. No transfers, except from local community colleges, are entertained for the Business School.

Wake Forest University

William Starling
Admissions Director
Winston Salem, NC 27109
(919) 761-5201

Transfer Applicants: 350
Admitted: 80

Articulation Agreements: None

On-Campus Housing: Not guaranteed
Room & Board: $3050

Tuition: $8800

Minimum Requirements: 2.0 GPA (see below)

Residency: 4 sems.

Mid-Year: On a space-available basis

Deadlines: Feb. 1 (Fall)
Oct. 15 (Spring)

Additional Comments:
Wake Forest expects transfer candidates to have greater than a 3.0 GPA. Most transfers accepted have a 3.3+ GPA, rank in the top 5% of their high school graduating class, and have a combined score above 1200 on the SAT.

Wellesley College

Kelly Walter
Director of Admissions
Wellesley, MA 02181
(617) 431-1183

Transfer Coordinator: Wendy Sibert

Transfer Applicants: 163
Admitted: 73

Articulation Agreements: None

On-Campus Housing: Guaranteed
Room & Board: $4660

Tuition: $12,300

Minimum Requirements: 3.4 to 3.5 GPA

Residency: Two academic years, which equals 4 sems.

Mid-Year: Yes

Deadlines: Feb. 1 (Fall)
Nov. 15 (Spring)

Additional Comments:
Wellesley offers a visiting student program through the Center for Continuing Education. Participants are expected to return to their original schools. Wellesley is also a member of the 12 College Exchange. Interviews are required for transfers.

Wesleyan University

Karl Furstenberg
Dean of Admissions
Middletown, CT 06457
(203) 347-9411

Transfer Applicants: 375–450
Admitted: 80–120

Articulation Agreements: None

On-Campus Housing: Guaranteed
Room & Board: $4775

Tuition: $15,185

Minimum Requirements: (see below)

Residency: 4 sems.

Mid-Year: Yes

Deadlines: March 1 (Fall)
Nov. 1 (Spring)

Additional Comments:
Wesleyan requires the high school and college transcript, SAT or ACT, but no Achievements. 60% of admitted applicants have a GPA greater than 3.5 and median SAT scores of 610 verbal, 650 math.

Wichita State University

Neill Sanders
Director of Admissions
Wichita, KS 67208
(316) 689-3085

Transfer Applicants: 2165
Admitted: 1588

Articulation Agreements: With all Kansas community
colleges

On-Campus Housing: Guaranteed
Room & Board: $2550

Tuition: $1422 in state
$3852 out of state

Minimum Requirements: 2.0 GPA

Residency: (see below)

Mid-Year: Yes

Deadlines: Rolling Admissions

Additional Comments:
Wichita State University accepts transfer students for all classes. Transfers from two-year colleges must complete 60 credit hours in residence. Students from four-year colleges need only finish the last 30.

Williams College

Phillip Smith
Director of Admissions
Williamstown, MA 01267
(413) 597-2211

Transfer Applicants: 200+
Admitted: Fewer than 20

Articulation Agreements: Williams cooperates with Berkshire Community College in Pittsfield, MA

On-Campus Housing: Guaranteed
Room & Board: $4664

Tuition: $14,135

Minimum Requirements: 3.5 GPA in a strong liberal arts program

Residency: 4 sems.

Mid-Year: Yes

Deadlines: March 1 (Fall)
Dec. 1 (Spring)

Additional Comments:
Williams gives preference to nontraditional students and community college graduates. The college is looking for transfers who demonstrate extremely high academic performance or who would add significantly to the diversity. Williams participates in the 12 College Exchange.

Yale University

Worth David
Dean of Admissions
New Haven, CT 06520
(203) 432-1900

Transfer Applicants: 670
Admitted: 30

Articulation Agreements: None

On-Campus Housing: Guaranteed
Room & Board: $5100

Tuition: $12,960

Minimum Requirements: None

Residency: 18 courses

Mid-Year: No

Deadlines: March 10

Index

INDEX